# CONTENTS

## Southern, Western & Eastern England

B...f...elds

AND

ND

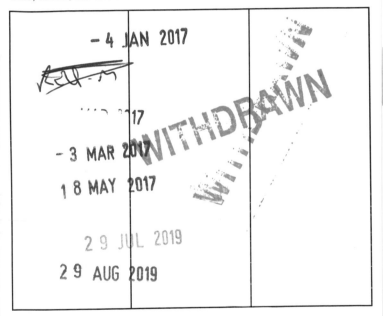

AMBERLEY

# ACKNOWLEDGEMENTS

Thanks are due to Shire books for allowing me to reprint *Discovering Battlefields of England and Scotland* with many updates and three new battle sites in Scotland. Thanks also to David Walker and his son David for information on Aberdeen, to the staff of the National Army Museum and to Robert Wake of York Castle Museum for useful photographs, to my son for taking command of the photographs, to Major R. W. Naesmyth of Posso, R A, (Rtd), for photographs and advice on Roundway Down, to Bernard Lowry for a wet day in Shrewsbury and some photographs, to Sally McLeod for two Scottish diagrams, to Sallyann for preparing the manuscript, to Carol Moonie and Lauren Potts for the Harlaw photograph and to my wife, as ever, for much support.

First published 2016

Amberley Publishing
The Hill, Stroud
Gloucestershire, GL5 4EP

www.amberley-books.com

British Library Cataloguing in Publication Data.
A catalogue record for this book is available from the British Library.

ISBN 978 1 4456 6214 5 (print)
ISBN 978 1 4456 6215 2 (ebook)

Origination by Amberley Publishing.
Printed in Great Britain.

# INTRODUCTION

Based on my *Discovering Battlefields of England and Scotland*, this book is an updated version of my Shire Books 1998 edition. There are some new battlefields – Montrose's (Old) Inverlochy and Tippermuir as well as Aberdeen so that we now have a total of seventy-nine battlefields. Some archaeological work has been done at Bosworth, so the actual battlefield has moved a bit and Killiecrankie has revealed a line of bullets further up the hill from where I had considered the battle took place. Was this because the Mackay infantry had muskets with plug-in bayonets and they realised that as soon as the Scots charged then they would have to resort to bayonets as there would not be time to reload?

Bosworth has also revealed its artillery barrage, some way from Ambien Hill, so my map has had to be redrawn. Like most early battles I don't think the artillery did much damage apart from making a noise, as reloading would have taken ages. Bannockburn battlefield has become an 'experience' with lots of flashing lights and a first-class restaurant, which makes it still worth a visit when (as happened with me) it is pouring with rain.

English Heritage have revamped their Hastings site so schools organising visits should make this a certainty. For information about re-enactments it is advisable to contact English Heritage at Swindon or the National Trust for Scotland at Edinburgh. Useful addresses are given at the end in the bibliograpy.

Enjoy visiting our battlefields.

John Kinross
Hereford

# LOCATIONS OF BATTLE SITES

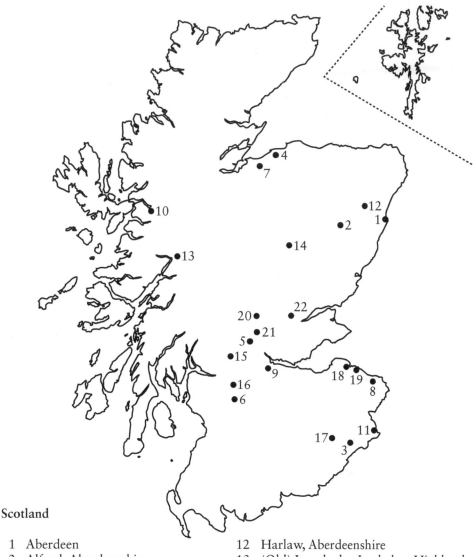

## Scotland

## Northern England & Midlands

| | | | |
|---|---|---|---|
| 23 | Adwalton Moor, Yorkshire | 38 | Naseby, Northamptonshire |
| 24 | Blore Heath, Staffordshire | 39 | Neville's Cross, Co.Durham |
| 25 | Boroughbridge, Yorkshire | 40 | Newark, Nottinghamshire |
| 26 | Bosworth, Leicestershire | 41 | Newburn Ford, Northumberland |
| 27 | Clifton Moor, Cumbria | 42 | Northampton |
| 28 | Edgecote, Northamptonshire | 43 | Otterburn, Northumberland |
| 29 | Edgehill, Warwickshire | 44 | Preston, Lancashire |
| 30 | Evesham, Worcestershire | 45 | Rowton Heath, Cheshire |
| 31 | Flodden, Northumberland | 46 | Shrewsbury, Shropshire |
| 32 | Hedgeley Moor, Northumberland | 47 | Stamford Bridge, Yorkshire |
| 33 | Homildon Hill, Northumberland | 48 | Stoke Field, Nottinghamshire |
| 34 | Marston Moor, Yorkshire | 49 | The Standard, Yorkshire |
| 35 | Mortimer's Cross, Herefordshire | 50 | Towton, Yorkshire |
| 36 | Myton, Yorkshire | 51 | Wakefield, Yorkshire |
| 37 | Nantwich, Cheshire | 52 | Worcester |

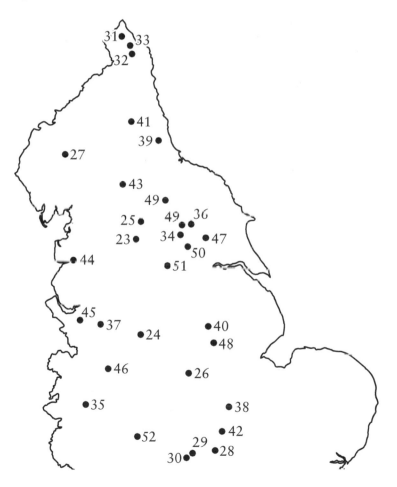

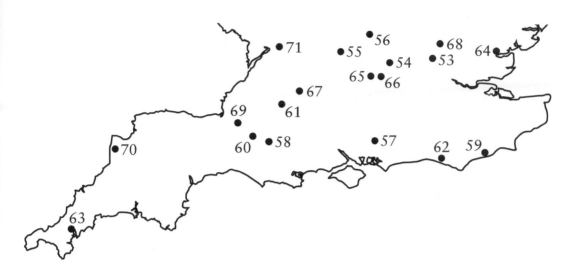

## Southern, Western and Eastern England

53  Barnet, Hertfordshire
54  Ashdown, Berkshire
55  Chalgrove Field, Oxfordshire
56  Cropredy Bridge, Oxfordshire
57  Cheriton, Hampshire
58  Ethandun, Wiltshire
59  Hastings, Sussex
60  Langport, Somerset
61  Lansdown Hill, Somerset
62  Lewes, Sussex

63  Lostwithiel, Cornwall
64  Maldon, Essex
65  Newbury I, Berkshire
66  Newbury II, Berkshire
67  Roundway Down, Wiltshire
68  St Albans, Hertfordshire
69  Sedgemoor, Somerset
70  Stratton, Cornwall
71  Tewkesbury, Gloucestershire

☐  **Foot soldiers**

◪  **Cavalry**

═  **Roads existing now and at time of battle**

╌  **Roads built since time of battle**

Key to the symbols used in the battle plans.

# SCOTLAND

## 1. ABERDEEN, 13 SEPTEMBER 1644

OS38 (925 045)

After his success at Tippermuir, Montrose moved up to attack Aberdeen before the forces of Argyll could catch him up. His force was still small – 70 horse and 1,500 foot. His opponent had 2,000 foot and 500 cavalry. In charge was Lord Balfour of Burleigh. The scene was set on the road between Upper Mills and Aberdeen. There was marshy ground behind Montrose's position and Burleigh was close to the road. The messenger sent to the Aberdeen magistrates was accompanied by a child drummer – a popular lad with the Royalist soldiers. One of Burleigh's men shot the lad on his way back to Montrose. Alasdair and the Irish were promised the sack of Aberdeen after the battle was won. Some of the Covenant foot and horse, unobserved at first, made their way through cottages on their right towards Montrose's left. Nathaniel Gordon's small bunch of horse kept them at bay and was reinforced by Rollo's horse from the other wing. Burleigh's left wing now charged, led by Forbes' horse. The Irish let them through, then turned round and fired at them as they turned to come back.

The Covenanters broke and fled for the safety of Aberdeen. For three days the sack of Aberdeen continued. Montrose went to his tent and took no part in it, thinking of the drummer boy. Some local women were carried off by the Irish, but were all released after Philiphaugh.

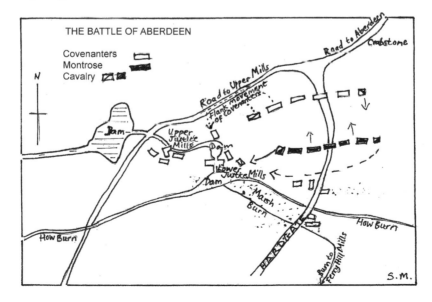

Argyll came to the rescue on 19 September, but by then Montrose had moved on to Badenoch, where he went down with fever, but recovering he made for Fyvie Castle, seat of the Earls of Dunfermline. Here his small force recovered – Alasdair had not rejoined but some of the Irish were with him under Magnus O'Cahan. Bullets were scarce and the pewter vessels in the castle were used for making bullets. Argyll withdrew after a successful charge by the Irish. Some of Montrose's lowland officers deserted to join Argyll. In need of more men and supplies, Montrose made his way back to join up with Alasdair at Blair Atholl.

Aberdeen was a disaster for Montrose. Until then he had fought a civilised series of battles but after Aberdeen many of his supporters thought of their future and shied away.

Fyvie Castle belongs to the National Trust for Scotland.
Tel. 01651 891266. Garden open all year. Castle, shop and tearoom. Open end of March to the end of October.

## Aberdeen Today

The battle map is almost impossible to relate to present-day Aberdeen. The service road to Upper Mills is now Union Street and there is still a Hardgate. Montrose came up this windy road and positioned his army on the hill above what is now Union Street. I am indebted to David Walker and his son David (co-author of the *Pevsner Guide to Aberdeenshire: South and Aberdeen*, 2015) for this valuable information.

# 2. ALFORD, 2 JULY 1645

## Aberdeenshire OS Landranger 37 (562 167)

In Scotland, after his victory at Auldearn, the Marquis of Montrose turned to meet Lieutenant General William Baillie, who, with an army of around 2,000, had crossed the Dee and was blocking the Royalists' route to the south. Baillie had lost some of his best men to another Covenanter, Lindsay, who was raising a new army in Perth. Montrose, after resting his troops in Elgin, lost the Gordons, who went home to Strathbogie, where their land was threatened by Baillie's men. Montrose retired after threatening Lindsay and waited for reinforcements to arrive. He took up a strong position at Corgarff Castle on the Don. The Gordons returned under Lord Gordon when Montrose had moved to Pitlurg Castle near the Gordon seat of Huntly. Montrose's Irish were absent recruiting; nevertheless he decided to attack. Moving south again, Montrose took up a commanding position on Gallows Hill near the village of Alford. With a bog protecting his rear, Montrose calculated that Baillie would cross the Don at the ford of Boat of Forbes nearby.

Montrose placed the Gordons on his right and Viscount Aboyne's horse on his left, with the Highlanders in the centre and a small reserve under the Master of Napier behind.

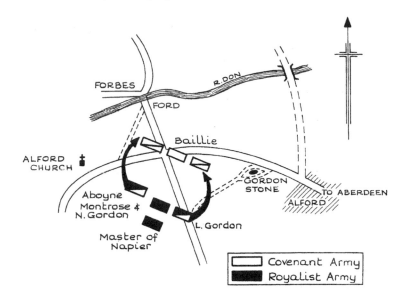

FORBES

R. DON

FORD

Baillie

ALFORD
CHURCH

GORDON
STONE

TO ABERDEEN

ALFORD

Aboyne
Montrose &
N. Gordon

L. Gordon

Master of
Napier

Covenant Army
Royalist Army

Aberdeen.

Baillie crossed the ford, led on by the impetuous Lord Balcarres, an experienced cavalry commander whose horse outnumbered Montrose's horse by nearly two to one. Infuriated that Baillie's army had taken so much of his family's cattle, young Lord Gordon led his right wing forward immediately. Balcarres's line broke but reformed, and a cavalry battle ensued, which was joined by Nathaniel Gordon's foot, who threw down their muskets and hacked at the enemy's horses with their swords. Aboyne led his horse around the opposing wing, which fled, leaving the Covenanters' centre pressed on all sides. Most fought where they stood and Balcarres and Baillie escaped with a few survivors.

Lord Gordon charged the retreating cavalry once too often and was shot from behind. The battle was a clear victory for Montrose but he lost his friend and gallant cavalry commander. With the exception of Lindsay's raw army, there was no one left for Montrose to beat in Scotland. But Naseby had been fought in June and the king's army in the south had dwindled, while that of Cromwell was only just beginning to recognise its new leader.

Castle of Corgarff. (Aberdeen Journals Ltd)

## Alford Today

Alford village, which is 25 miles (40 km) west of Aberdeen on the A944, is modern and the site of the battle is the crossroads on the far side of the village – the river was much wider in those days. Gallows Hill is the height above the crossroads. A new road leads to the Gordon Stone, which is railed off at the edge of a field and looks as if it has been there much longer than the battle date. The battlefield symbol (crossed swords) on the Ordnance Survey map is not on the generally agreed site of the battle.

# 3. ANCRUM MOOR, 27 FEBRUARY 1545

## Scottish Borders OS Landranger 74 (619 272)

Henry VIII was especially bitter towards Scotland at the end of his reign. The Pope had appointed Archbishop Beaton of St Andrews as one of his cardinals, and the Scots had rejected Henry's proposal of the marriage of his son Edward to the infant Mary, Queen of Scots. In addition to this, he was at war with France and could not afford to let the 'auld alliance' of France and Scotland develop.

The Earl of Hertford was sent to raid Scotland. 'Spoil and turn upside down the cardinal's town of St Andrews, as the upper stone may be the nether,' went the instructions from the king, 'sparing no creature alive.' After landing at Leith, the English

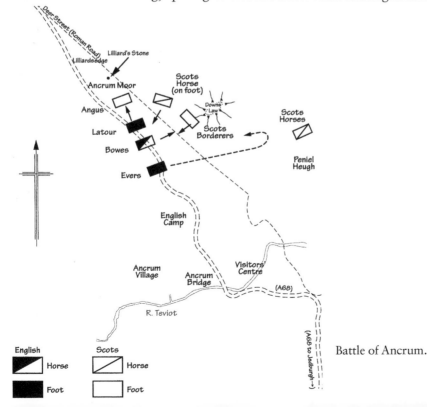

Battle of Ancrum.

carried out these harsh orders and even pillaged Edinburgh. The weak Earl of Arran was not able to raise an army, but in the borders the Earl of Angus, recently recalled from exile, had seen his estates ravaged by two English knights, Sir Ralph Evers and Sir Brian Latoun. In 1545 these two led an army of 5,000, of whom 3,000 were foreign mercenaries and 800 broken Scottish clans, into Scotland by way of Jedburgh. Melrose Abbey was pillaged and the graves of the Douglases were desecrated. On his way back to Jedburgh by the Roman road, camping at Ancrum village, Evers saw movements on the hill known as Peniel Heugh. He noticed the Scottish horse retreating and gave the order to attack. The English were overloaded with booty and, when they had struggled up the hill, they found the Scottish Army in a hollow calmly awaiting the attack. The sun, the wind and the smoke from the arquebuses obscured the English banners so that the mercenaries did not know friend from foe, especially as 800 borderers changed sides and joined Angus's line. The Scots horses had been put deliberately on the hill, but their cavalry fought on foot. Evers wasted time and energy climbing the hill after them.

Armed with the Jedburgh axe, a terrifying weapon consisting of a billhook on one side and a metal hook on the other, the Scots set upon the cavalry of Latoun and Bowes, pulling riders from their horses and stabbing them on the ground. With cries of 'remember Broomhouse', the Scottish spearmen advanced (Broomhouse was a tower burnt by the English with its lady and her family inside). Evers' Scottish troops mostly deserted to Angus' army. Latoun's cavalry fled through the second and third lines. Evers and Latoun were killed. Nearly 1,000 men were captured, while the Scottish losses were small. The town of Jedburgh was freed from the English, the wagon train was captured and the abbey of Coldingham, which had been fortified by the English, was regained.

Ancrum was a decisive victory and one that helped to unify Scotland, for Angus had been under suspicion of being in the pay of Henry VIII. Henry had fresh worries, for in the summer of the same year, spurred on by the Scottish success, the French landed 2,000 men in the Isle of Wight and Annebaut's fleet attacked Portsmouth.

Maiden Lilliard's tomb. (Robson)

## Ancrum Moor Today

The battlefield is simple to find because Peniel Heugh has the large Waterloo Tower on the top, visible from the A68 a few miles north of Jedburgh. On the line of the Roman road is the tomb of Maiden Lilliard, bearing the following inscription:

> Fair maiden Lilliard lies under this
> Little was her stature, but muckle was her fame;
> Upon the English loons she laid many thumps,
> And when her legs were cuttit off,
> She fought upon her stumps.

According to tradition, Lilliard's lover had been killed by the English and she drove into their ranks with a sword, continuing to fight when her legs had been cut off by Evers' men. To reach the tomb, turn off the A68 at the Maxton sign and take the footpath signs for St Cuthbert's Way, immediately on the right from the junction. The chapel-like building on Down's Law, Baron's Folly, has no connection with the battle.

Alternative approach for walkers: There is a new visitor centre at Ancrum, just at the foot of the Waterloo monument. This is Harestanes Countryside Visitor Centre, which has free parking, a café, toilets and a shop. The St Cuthbert's Way (going backwards) crosses the B6400 through a wood and then straight down Dere Street to Lilliardsedge getting to the Maiden Lilliard monument safely after 2 miles.

# 4. AULDEARN, 9 MAY 1645

## Highland OS Landranger 27 (918 550)

James Graham, Marquis of Montrose, was Charles I's lieutenant general for Scotland. After a fruitless campaign in the Lowlands in the spring of 1644, he moved north again in the summer to recruit support and, with help from Ireland and the Macdonalds, waged a successful war on the Covenant armies. In February 1645 he defeated the Campbells at Inverlochy and Parliamentary forces under General William Baillie and Colonel Sir John Hurry were sent to defeat him. Montrose entered Dundee, where his exhausted troops replenished their supplies, and left with the enemy hard on his heels. By devious tracks he reach Speyside and, when he became aware of Hurry's army in front of him, he followed it towards Inverness where there were Covenant reinforcements. Stopping at the little village of Auldearn, Montrose arranged his men during the early hours on 9 May. He placed Macdonald's Irishmen of Antrim, who numbered around 500, in a thin line in front of the village, with one wing on the castle hill where the present Boath Doocot stands, and his cavalry of 200 in two groups under Lord Lewis Gordon and Lord Aboyne were partly hidden by a hill. His own group of 800 men was next to the cavalry and a few musketeers held the thin centre where the standard was placed. Hurry had nearly 4,000 foot and 400 cavalry but he

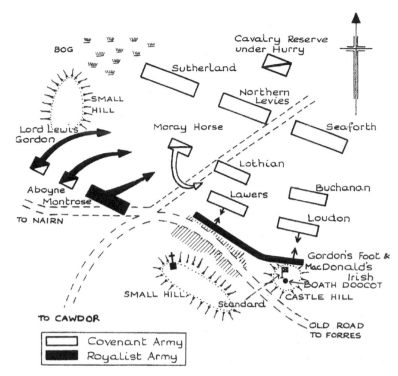

BOG

Cavalry Reserve
under Hurry

Sutherland

SMALL
HILL

Northern
Levies

Lord Lewis
Gordon

Moray Horse

Seaforth

Lothian

Aboyne

Lawers

Buchanan

Montrose

Loudon

TO NAIRN

Gordon's Foot &
MacDonald's
Irish
BOATH DOOCOT
CASTLE HILL

SMALL HILL

Standard

TO CAWDOR

OLD ROAD
TO FORRES

Covenant Army
Royalist Army

Battle of Auldearn.

Auldearn: the Boath Doocot. (National Trust for
Scotland)

could not position them properly because, marching from Nairn, he had spotted the
boggy ground (it had been raining for several days) and as a result his regiments had to
deploy. He sent Lawers' men ahead with the Moray horse under Major Drummond in
support on the right. Loudon's regiment advanced on the left and Buchanan and others
followed behind with Hurry taking up the rear with his reserve cavalry.

The Irish, with their backs to stone walls and enclosures, advanced and fought
manfully. Gradually, fighting against huge odds, they were forced back. A messenger
arrived at Montrose's wing asking for help. 'Will you let the Macdonalds have all the
glory of the day?' said Montrose to Lord Gordon and the two troops of Royalist cavalry,

who were hidden from the enemy, charged Hurry's right wing. Major Drummond gave the wrong order in the confusion and the Moray horse wheeled the wrong way, cutting down some of the Lothian regiment. Lord Lewis Gordon's horsemen drove the remnants of Drummond's horse off the field but Aboyne wheeled right and charged the exposed flank of the Lothian and Lawers regiments. Montrose pressed against Buchanan and Loudon. The Irish joined the fight and Hurry, anxious to save his reserves, withdrew to Inverness. Drummond was tried and shot as a traitor in Inverness.

In England, the Earl of Leven's Scottish Army in Yorkshire withdrew to Westmorland to prevent Charles I from linking up with Montrose, and Hurry withdrew to join Baillie. It was not a decisive victory but tactically was probably the most brilliant of all Montrose's successes. Around 2,000 Covenanters and a few hundred Royalists were killed.

## Auldearn Today

The National Trust for Scotland preserves the Boath Doocot at Auldearn. Nearby, the Trust has erected a viewpoint where there is a plaque with an excellent plan and description of the battle. What is confusing is that the main road between Nairn and Forres (A96) is new and the old road no longer exists. If the Macdonalds had posted a man on the castle mound they would have had a commanding view and Montrose must have taken a risk running the battle from the left wing where it would have been difficult to see exactly what was happening.

# 5. BANNOCKBURN, 24 JUNE 1314

## Stirling OS Landranger 57 (393 669)

An English victory at Dunbar in 1296 over the Scots, who had ousted Edward I's puppet king Balliol, was the beginning of the Scottish War of Independence. When Wallace was defeated two years later by Edward's army at Falkirk, the Scots looked to another leader, Robert Bruce. The tide of fortune turned slowly, but in 1307 Edward I died and his successor, Edward II, was not the brilliant soldier his father had been. In March 1306 Bruce had disposed of his rival Comyn and crowned himself king of Scotland at Scone. Edward allowed the situation to deteriorate, and by 1313 the English garrisons at Perth, Dumfries, Edinburgh and Roxburgh had surrendered and Mowbray had agreed to surrender Stirling to Edward Bruce, Robert's brother, by Midsummer Day 1314 unless he was relieved by an English army.

The Scots arranged a gathering at Torwood near Stirling as Edward's army of 22,000 marched through Edinburgh towards Stirling. Bruce's army was around 8,000 strong, of which 5,000 were spearmen armed with 12-foot (3.6-metre) spears and steel helmets; 500 were lightly armed horsemen and a few were archers. The Scots were in five groups under Robert and Edward Bruce, Sir James Douglas and Sir Thomas Randolph, Earl of Moray, with Sir Robert Keith commanding the horsemen.

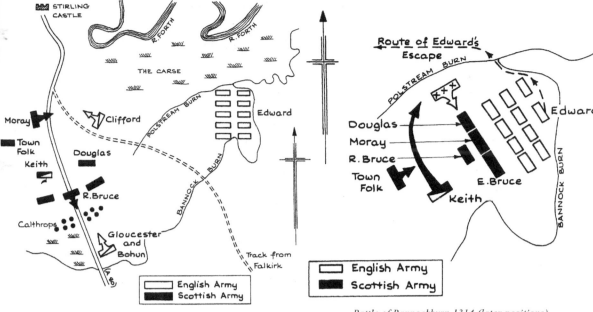

*Battle of Bannockburn, 1314 (first positions).*

*Battle of Bannockburn, 1314 (later positions).*

The English knights were heavily armoured and their horses were weighed down by the impedimenta of an army on the march. Bruce withdrew his men to the New Park, a thick wood on the edge of the little River Bannock blocking the Falkirk–Stirling road. He dug concealed pits and covered the ground with calthrops (spikes to prevent the passage of horses) and then waited for his enemy.

The younger English knights, arriving at the Bannock on 23 June, immediately pressed forward to attack the outnumbered Scots. Sir Henry Bohun spotted Bruce himself and drove his horse at him with his lance levelled. Dodging to one side, the king of the Scots brought down his heavy axe and shattered both axe and Bohun's helmet with one mighty blow. The English vanguard withdrew demoralised. The Scots were exultant.

Early next morning the Scottish spearmen advanced in their densely packed formations called schiltrons. The English were in low-lying marshland between the Polstream and the Bannock burns. Edward hastily ordered the Earl of Gloucester and his horsemen to attack. The Scots had been trained to kill the horses first so that the heavy English knights would be helpless. It was a cruelly effective plan and was used by the clansmen at Prestonpans 400 years later. Young Gloucester was one of the first to fall and he was followed by Clifford, Sir Edmund de Manley, Sir Pain Tiptoft and many other English knights. When they reached the flank, where they checked the spearmen for a time, Keith's horsemen cut them down.

The Scots were still outnumbered but many of the English could not reach the front ranks to fight. Suddenly a small army of townsfolk from Stirling entered the fray. Armed with home-made weapons and waving blanket banners, they cut off the stragglers. Edward, wielding his battleaxe, had his horse killed under him but was rescued by his bodyguard, who took him safely to Dunbar and Berwick. One of them, Sir Giles d'Argentan, refused to escape and plunged his horse into the nearest schiltron. 'I am not accustomed to fly,' he said, 'nor shall I do so now.'

The flight of their king was the signal for panic. The English fled back through the Bannock, where many were killed and trampled on. Several hundred were drowned in the Forth or killed by the country folk. Aylmer de Valence, Lord Pembroke, the man

Bannockburn: the battlefield
and the burn. (Author)

Bannockburn: the battle cairn.
(ARN Kinross)

who had beaten Bruce and Methven eight years before, succeeded in escaping with the Welsh archers to Carlisle. Bruce was generous to his prisoners and let many go free. His own men were rewarded with the captured English spoil. A wheelwright from Stirling, a young man called Kinross, who was one of the last to arrive at the action, was granted land in the town. Mowbray, the governor of the castle, was received as a friend in Bruce's camp. Scotland had won her independence for a time and England had suffered her first defeat since Hastings.

## Bannockburn Today

Bannockburn is a few miles south of Stirling on the A80 and is preserved by the National Trust for Scotland. Bruce's position on the first day of the battle is now marked by a fine statue of him mounted on his charger. The statue was made by Charles d'Orville Pilkington Jackson and unveiled by the queen in 1964. Adjacent to it are a massive flagpole and a battle cairn with a commemorative plaque. The heritage centre nearby has an excellent audio-visual interpretation of the whole battle in its auditorium. To book in advance for the 'Experience' go to www.battleofbannockburn. com. There is a car park and restaurant, but for those wanting to see the original burn, stout shoes and an umbrella are necessary; I was unable to find it.

# 6. BOTHWELL BRIDGE, 22 JUNE 1679

North Lanarkshire, OS Landranger 64 (711578)

Charles II restored the bishops to Scotland and the Episcopacy, which replaced the Presbyterian system of church governance. The Duke of Lauderdale enforced the law, and all prayer meetings of the Covenanters had to be held out of doors, with sentries posted to give warnings in the event of royal troops.

At Drumclog near Strathaven, in June 1679, the Life Guards under John Graham of Claverhouse, later Viscount Dundee, were outnumbered in a bog by the Covenanters led by Sir Robert Hamilton, Lord Balfour of Burleigh and David Hackston of Rathillet. Thirty-eight were killed and Dundee narrowly escaped in the nick of time, with his horse mortally wounded. Charles II, on hearing of the disaster, put the Scottish loyalists under the command of his illegitimate son, the Duke of Monmouth, who had recently seen service in Holland, and with only four troops of cavalry joined Dundee in Falkirk. The Earl of Linlithgow was in command of the foot, many of whom were militia, and on 22 June Monmouth reached Bothwell on the road to Hamilton, where the rebels, commanded by their preachers, had defended the bridge, which was 120 feet (36 metres) long and had a central fortified gateway and was paved with stones from the Clyde beneath.

Monmouth's Macfarlanes charged the bridge, which was held by Rathillet's marksmen. The ammunition of the defenders soon ran out. They fell back, and the Lennox Highlanders crossed the bridge followed by Dundee and the cavalry, which soon put the rebels to flight, exacting cruel revenge for their fellow soldiers killed at Drumclog. The Covenanters fled to Hamilton, which was partially defended by Balfour of Burleigh and their 2,000 horse commanded by Sir Robert Hamilton. The other leaders, Russell and Barscobe, went to Cumlock with their followers, and thence a few escaped to Holland.

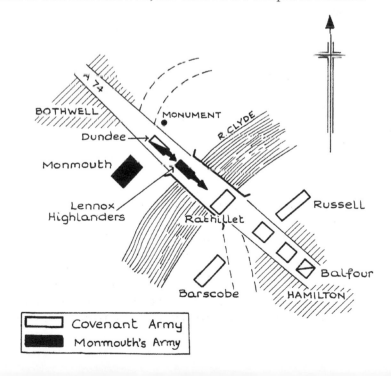

Bothwell Bridge: the present bridge over the Clyde. (Author)

In all 1300 prisoners were taken and shut up in Greyfriars churchyard at Edinburgh. Most were freed when they signed a bond giving up the Covenant. Those that refused were shipped to the colonies. Two hundred were drowned off Orkney and others died in the dreadful conditions at Leith prior to their departure.

The Duke of Monmouth took pity on the Covenanters and tried to prevent any recriminations, but shortly after this he fell out of favour. The bravery of the defenders of the bridge was not lost on him however, and six years later similar untrained peasants formed his army at Sedgemoor.

## Bothwell Bridge Today

The battlefield can be visted on the A47 between Glasgow and Hamilton. The modern bridge has a monument on the Bothwell bank, which was erected at the beginning of the twentieth century. It is a rusticated obelisk to the memory of the Covenanters and stands on the Clyde Walkway footpath. Monmouth is supposed to have occupied the highest point above the ridge.

# 7. CULLODEN, 16 APRIL 1746

## Highland OS Landranger 27 (736 452)

The 'scrambled affair' of Falkirk and the replacement of Hawley by the young Duke of Cumberland with veterans from Fontenoy persuaded the Jacobites to pull back to Inverness. En route the heavy guns were abandoned at Perth – some of the ones captured after Prestonpans had already been lost in the snow over Shap, and at Levens Hall today there is some cannon ammunition from a fallen Jacobite ammunition wagon. Detachments of Highlanders went to Sutherland to collect French gold; another group captured a government post at Fort Augustus and a third besieged Fort William.

When Cumberland crossed the Spey, arriving at Nairn on 14 April 1746, he had been unopposed. Murray planned a night attack on their position but only 3 miles

Key. Jacobite army: A, Macdonalds and Duke of Perth; B, Farquharsons, Macleans, Macintoshes, Frasers, Stewarts of Appin, Camerons; C, Lord George Murray's Atholl Brigade; D, Irish under Brigadier Stapleton; E, Lord Drummond's Royal Scots, Lord Lewis Gordon; F, Ogilvy Regiment; G, Fitzjames Horse and Life Guards; H, Reserve under Lord Balmerino. Hanoverian army: 1, Cobham's Dragoons, Kingston's Horse; 2, Pulteney, Royal Scots; 3, Cholmondeley, Price, Royal Scots Fusiliers; 4, Munro, Barrel; 5, Wolfe; 6, Battereau, Howard, Fleming; 7, Bligh, Sempill, Ligonier; 8, Blakeney. The Duke Cumberland is positioned in front of Howard's Regiment, and the Prince behind the Fitzjames Horse.

*Battle of Culloden, 1746.*

short of their camp the warning drum sounded and the weary Highlanders had to retreat back to Drummossie Moor. Here next day the final battle took place in driving snow. It was not an ideal battlefield. The 4,600 Highlanders were outnumbered two to one, their flanks covered by walls which would mean the Royal cavalry could charge round unseen and the Macdonalds, usually on the right wing, were put on the left.

The cannonade that started the battle lasted fifteen minutes and the Royal gunners were able to knock out most of the Jacobite guns. Barrel's and Munro's regiments were cut down but Wolfe moved his men so they could fire at a flank. The Irish pickets under Colonel Stapleton fought bravely and kept out the dragoons and Kingston Horse until their leader was killed.

Cumberland's orders are still extant. He encouraged the men to attack the undefended side of the Highlanders, who always carried their targes of the left arm so they could wield claymores with their right arms. This plan worked well. Most of the Highland chiefs escaped but Lord Balmerino was captured by young Lieutenant Tudor (see the Tudor papers in Aylesbury Library) who became an ADC to Cumberland. His Lordship was later executed in London.

Culloden: the battle cairn. (Author)

Charles escaped, led by members of Fitzjames horse and when the battle ended, 200 Highlanders had been killed with the Royal army losing 364. It was in the brutal follow-up to Inverness that a further 2,000 were killed, many wounded being killed where they lay down. The nation was horrified by the cruel harrying of the glens afterwards. 'Nothing like his (Cumberland's) measure had been known,' writes Lang, 'since the cruelties of Henry VIII on the Border.'

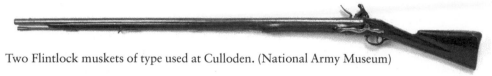

Two Flintlock muskets of type used at Culloden. (National Army Museum)

## Culloden Today

The battlefield of Culloden belongs to the National Trust for Scotland and is clearly signposted a few miles from Inverness just off the A9. In 1984 a visitor centre was opened by Colonel Donald Cameron of Lochiel, twenty-sixth chief of the Clan Cameron. The centre has a bookshop, a reading room with a selection of books on the Jacobites, a circular display room with drawings of the battle and the aftermath, a video cinema and a restaurant.

For details of charges and opening times, phone 01463 796090.

# 8. DUNBAR, 3 SEPTEMBER 1650

East Lothian OS Landranger 67 (702 758)

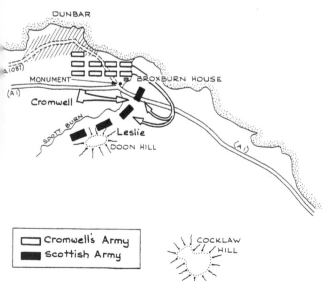

*Left*: Battle of Dunbar.
*Below*: Dunbar Battle stone. (Author)

After the execution of Charles I, his son was proclaimed king in Scotland (the Covenanters forced him to sign their document upholding Presbyterianism). The Marquis of Argyll, who a few months before had executed the unfortunate Marquis of Montrose after his defeat at Carbisdale, set about building an army to conquer the English forces under Oliver Cromwell. With David Leslie, Cromwell's former ally at Marston Moor, as its leader, the Scottish Army consisted of 'ministers' sons, clerks and such who hardly ever saw or heard of any sword but that of the spirit'.

With the Navy to support him, Cromwell moved up towards Edinburgh, where Leslie checked him by constructing entrenchments from Holyrood to Leith. In August 1650, Cromwell, based at Dunbar, put his main force on Doon Hill, where it could watch the enemy and block the escape route at Cockburnspath and Ewieside Hill. Cromwell remarked, 'we are upon an engagement very difficult'. With disease in his army, Cromwell knew he must attack. Leslie withdrew on 2 September and lined his army up on the Spott burn near Broxburn.

Setting out before dawn on the 3 September, six cavalry regiments, commanded by Charles Fleetwood, Edward Whalley and John Lambert, with George Monck's three infantry regiments, attacked the Scots over the burn. The Scots had extinguished the match used to light their muskets because of the night rain. They put up a stiff resistance in spite of this, but Cromwell's own regiment 'did come seasonably in and at push of pike did repel the stoutest regiment the enemy had there'. The second cavalry charge 'made the Lord of Hosts as stubble to our swords'. Forcing their way through the gap by the sea, the English turned and caught Leslie's main force in the rear. Nearly 3,000 were killed or wounded and twice that number captured.

Edinburgh fell to the victorious Cromwell and Leslie withdrew to Stirling. The religious leaders said that the defeat was due to the estrangement of the Lord from an army that fought for an unconverted king. Leslie's final thrust the following year at Worcester also failed. That battle was fought on the anniversary of Dunbar.

## Dunbar Today

Take the A1087 to Dunbar from the A1(T), signed to the cement works. A battle stone is in a walled alcove on the right of the road. It is inscribed with the words of Thomas Carlyle: 'Here took place the brunt or essential agony of the battlefield below.'

# 9. FALKIRK, 17 JANUARY 1746

## Falkirk OS Landranger 65 (875 790)

The retreat of the Jacobites from Derby did not mean the immediate end of 'the Forty-five'. Edinburgh was back in government hands, and so too was Stirling Castle, but Perth was the rallying point of Jacobite reinforcements, some of whom had sailed from France into Montrose unopposed. In January 1746 Prince Charles Edward

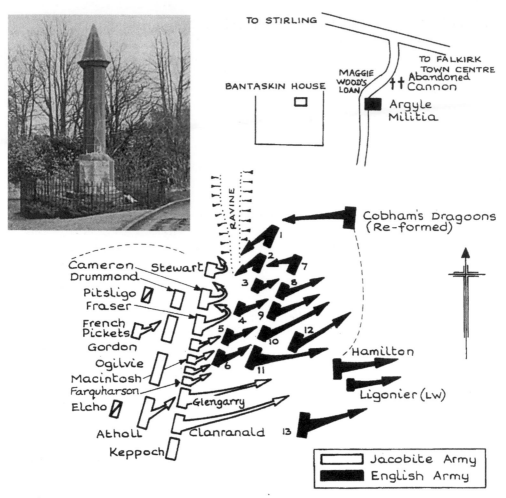

*Above:* Key. English army: 1, Ligonier (RW); 2, Price; 3, Royals; 4, Pulteney; 5, Cholmondeley; 6, Wolfe, 7 Barrel; 8, Battereau; 9 Fleming; 10, Munro; 11, Blakeney; 12, Howard; 13, Glasgow Volunteers. Jacobite army: the Macintosh company fought side by side with the Macphersons (left) and the Macknezies (right). *Inset*: Falkirk: the battle monument.

Stuart's army besieged Stirling Castle. In Edinburgh, General Henry Hawley took command of the infantry and dragoons, of which there were twelve regiments, nine having recently landed from Flanders. Hawley's one weakness was artillery. He had only a motley collection of guns from Edinburgh Castle, commanded by Captain Cunningham, who had to raise a scratch force of gunners from country people.

By 16 January Hawley's army had camped at Falkirk. It numbered around 8,000 men, and the general's aide-de-camp, Stuart Mackenzie, has left a graphic picture of the ensuing battle in letter to Robert Trevor, which is preserved in the Trevor papers in the Buckinghamshire County Record Office.

Prince Charles' commander Lord George Murray had originally sent out Lord Elcho's cavalry to reconnoitre near Linlithgo, where he hoped to seize some stores. He was informed of Hawley's approach and on 15 January the Highlanders, around 9,000 in number now that the Perth reinforcements had come in, drew up in battle order on

Plean Muir 2 miles (3 km) south-east of Bannockburn. Murray saw the advantage of occupying the hill above Falkirk and sent his infantry there in two columns, the horse under Lord John Drummond taking the main road from Stirling, where the Duke of Perth was left with 1,000 men in the castle siege lines. On 17 January, while the Jacobites were on the move, Hawley was being entertained to breakfast at Callander House by the Countess of Kilmarnock. It was not until the afternoon that he realised the seriousness of the situation and ordered his army forward through the narrow Maggie Wood's Loan on to the hill.

Cunningham's cannon got stuck in a bog on their way up the hill and played no part in the engagement. The Jacobites were in three lines with the Macdonalds under Keppoch on the right, the Stewarts on the left and a deep ravine in front of their left. The right wing was protected by a bog. The government troops were in two lines with the Argyll Militia in reserve. In the centre were Hamilton's and Wolfe's regiments, and the driving rain and poor visibility did not encourage the men of Ligonier's dragoons, who were given the order to charge. Murray commanded the Jacobite right and gave the order to fire when the dragoons were a few yards off. The result was devastating, and Clanranald's men dashed into the fray. Hamilton's dragoons turned and fled, cutting a path through the newly raised Glasgow Volunteers. 'What hindered the rebels from pursuing our left, God knows,' wrote Mackenzie. Not one in twenty muskets would work because of the rain, and the Jacobites, who were more accustomed to using swords than muskets, charged across the ravine.

Unfortunately for the Jacobites there was no commander of their left wing and the three regiments of Price, Ligonier and Barrel stood firm and caught them in the flank. Cobham's dragoons reformed and came back up the hill but Murray had brought forward the Atholl regiment, who drove them off. Hawley was now off the field, and three pieces of Cunningham's artillery were salvaged, the rest falling into Jacobite hands.

'If the victory was to be given to either side', wrote Mackenzie, 'it certainly was theirs rather than ours; our loss and theirs I believe are pretty near equal.'

The surprising result of Falkirk was the retreat of the Highlanders. Instead of assuming a defensive position at Falkirk, they renewed the siege of Stirling Castle without success and retreated to Perth and Inverness. Cumberland took over command of the government army, and Culloden was not far away. Lord George Murray realised that the winter was unsuitable for keeping an army in the field and that they would do better in the spring. The number of deserters worried Murray, but Charles was anxious to hold his ground and to wait for further French reinforcements. It was Murray who had his way, so that Falkirk was merely a temporary halt to the government army. The man who laughed loudest at Hawley's defeat was Cope, who was £10,000 the richer after winning a bet that Hawley would meet the same fate that Cope himself had met much earlier at Prestonpans.

## Falkirk Today

The town of Falkirk is so industrialised that most of the battlefield has now been built on. However, Maggie Wood's Loan can easily be found on the Stirling road and there is a battle monument nearby erected in 1927. Take Lochgreen Road of Slamannan Road near Falkirk High station and the monument is on the right at a right-hand junction.

# 10. GLEN SHIEL, 10 JUNE 1719

## Highland OS Landranger 33 (991 133)

The 1715 rising cost of the Jacobite cause was nearly twelve million pounds, and by 1718 the supporters of James Stuart, the Old Pretender, had run out of money as the French pension paid to his mother, Mary of Modena, who died in May, was lost. The one hope of the Jacobites was Cardinal Giulio Alberoni of Spain, who was prompted by the Duke of Ormonde to raise a fleet and an armada to invade England. By early March 1719 it set sail with twenty-nine ships and 5,000 troops. The same misfortune hit this armada as its more famous predecessor – a storm. The ships were scattered and most returned home to Cadiz. However, two frigates with 300 Spanish troops under George Keith, Earl Marischal, left San Sebastian on 8 March and reached Lewis in April. They were joined by the Earl of Seaforth and the Marquis of Tullibardine. After argument over who was in command, Tullibardine organised the setting up of an arsenal in Eilean Donan Castle in Loch Duich. Keith sent the Spanish ships home, and it was not long before three English frigates appeared – the *Worcester*, under Captain Boyle, the *Enterprize* under Captain Herdman and the *Flamborough* under Captin Heldersley – and opened fire on the castle.

The Spaniards escaped with some of the arms and, joining Rob Roy's forces with around 1,500 Highlanders, mostly Mackenzies, Macraes, Macgregors and Murrays, proceeded to march round the loch and into the pass of Glen Shiel, where Seaforth, the Spaniards and Tullibardine took up a defensive position guarding the bridge.

General Wightman, who had been second in command of the government army at Sheriffmuir, was dispatched with around 1,100 men, including a Dutch regiment and four Coehorn mortars, to put down the rising. He drew up his men at Glen Shiel, facing the bridge, on 10 June. At around 5.00 p.m. his mortars opened fire and his regiment on the right wing found their way around the back of the Highlanders' line

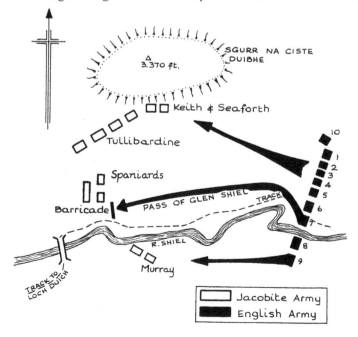

*Battle of Glen Shiel, 1719.*

Painting of Eilean Donan Castle.
(Painting by S. Innes)

and routed them. The Spaniards were made of sterner stuff and retired to another defensive position, finally agreeing to surrender the following day. Around twenty-one of Wightman's men were killed and 121 wounded. On the Jacobite side the losses were only ten killed. Keith was badly wounded but managed to escape and find his way to the continent. Seaforth was wounded by a grenade – Glen Shiel is one of the earliest examples of grenadiers in action – but he and Tullibardine also made their escape along with the young Lord George Murray. Thus ended 'the Nineteen'.

Mackintosh of Borlum:

In 1719 the commander of the Spanish force at Glen Shiel was Brigadier Mackintosh of Borlum, who had escaped from prison after his capture at Preston in 1715. Newly arrived from France, he again escaped. But he was recaptured in 1727 and confined to Edinburgh Castle, where he lived to the age of eighty-five. His wife, a former maid of

Glen Shiel. (M. D. Kinross)

honour to Queen Anne, was allowed to visit him in prison and they had a daughter, Winwood, a son Lachlan, who died before his father, and another son, Shaw. Shaw's son became a highwayman, he was the last of the family.

## Glen Shiel Today

The site of the battle is around half a mile (800 metres) east of the new bridge, and the grave of one of Montagu's officers is visible near a waterfall. Bullets are still occasionally found in the riverbed. Eilean Donan Castle, which was blown up by the *Worcester*, was restored by Colonel Macrae-Gilstrap in the 1920s. The Spaniards supposedly threw their treasure into a deep lochan nearby before they surrendered, but this is more legend than fact. The castle, home of the clan Macrae, is nearby and is open in summer. For details, telephone 01599 555202. www.eileandonancastle.com.

# 11. HALIDON HILL, 19 JULY 1333

Berwickshire OS Landranger 75 (972 548)

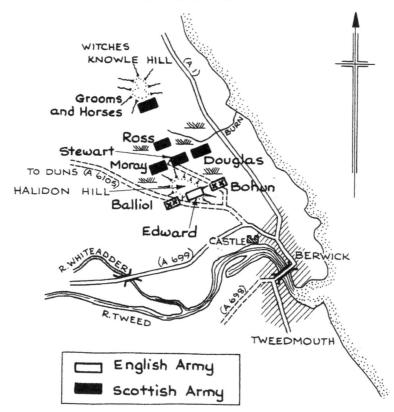

*Battle of Halidon Hill, 1333.*

When Edward III came to the throne in 1330 he was soon to face as much trouble from Scotland as his father, Edward II. Edward Balliol, a Scot with an equal claim to the Scottish throne as he was a cousin of the Bruces, took an expedition to Fife by sea and defeated the Scots at Dupplin Moor. In September 1332 Balliol was crowned at Scone but within a year the combined forces of the Earl of Moray and Archibald Douglas had driven him into the border country. Edward III gathered an army and, declaring void the Treaty of Northampton, which had agreed to recognise the sovereignty of Scotland, joined up with Balliol to besiege the walled town of Berwick-upon-Tweed.

Worn down by Edward's great siege engines, the defenders of Berwick agreed in June to surrender the town by 11 July if they were not relieved before that date. It was a situation similar to that of Stirling Castle before Bannockburn. The Scottish relieving force managed to cross the Tweed upstream and burn Tweedmouth. In the diversion 200 of them reached Berwick and the rest pushed on toward Bamburgh.

A new arrangement was made between the town and Edward that he would return the hostages by 20 July if 200 more Scots succeeded in getting through his lines. Douglas led his men back over the river to Duns and Edward, whose army consisted of 'murderers, robbers and poachers', posted them on the top of Halidon Hill, where he could overlook both the town and the direction from which Douglas would attack, and arranged them in three divisions with archers on each wing. The left was commanded by Balliol, the centre by Edward and the right wing by Sir Edward Bohun, the constable.

On 19th July the Scots approached from Duns. They were a larger army than Edward's, which had suffered from desertions, and were also arranged in three divisions under the Earl of Moray, Robert the Steward and Archibald Douglas. 200 picked men commanded by the Earl of Ross were in the rear. Waiting until the first wave of Scots were on the bog before Halidon, Edward's archers opened a devastating fire. Balliol's dismounted knights disposed of the few who reached them and the archers took a heavy toll of the second and third waves. Only Ross stood his ground and fought a rearguard action while the young Robert escaped. The English knights remounted and chased the Scots back to Duns, few of the latter being mounted as their horses had been seized by their frightened grooms who had watched their masters being defeated from Witches Knowle Hill. Seventy Scottish lords, including Douglas, 500 knights and several thousand foot soldiers were killed for the loss of one English knight, one man at arms and the Newcastle contingent, which arrived late and was cut down to a man.

Bannockburn had been avenged, but Scotland was still undefeated and Balliol, although restored, was never accepted by the Scots, who smuggled their young king, David II, to safety in France.

## Halidon Hill Today

Take the A6105 out of Berwick-upon-Tweed towards Duns. Turn right at the hotel and then left down an unmade road at the signpost pointing to the battle site. There is no monument, but a rough cairn marks the spot and an Ordnance Survey pointer stands on the crest of the hill. It is a commanding position worth visiting for the magnificent view in all directions.

# 12. HARLAW, 24 JULY 1411

Aberdeenshire OS Landranger 38 (752 242)

In Scotland the final struggle for supremacy between the Highlands and the Lowlands took place around 20 miles (32 km) north of Aberdeen. Today Harlaw is forgotten by historians, yet it was one of the bloodiest battles ever fought between Scots.

The death of King Robert III in 1406 and the capture of his son James by the English left Scotland in the hands of Robert Stewart, the first Duke of Albany. He was an ambitious statesman of considerable popularity, but he was tied to an English truce, for his own son, John, Earl of Buchan, was also a prisoner of England's Henry IV. Donald Macdonald, second Lord of the Isles, the Celtic chieftain, demanded the earldom of Ross from Albany but the latter refused as his own son had a better right to the earldom. In 1408, when Albany was turning to France, Donald made a treaty with Henry asking the English king to support his claim which would give him most of northern Scotland. Heading out from Ardtornish Castle on the Sound of Mull, Donald crossed to the mainland and augmented his force of islanders from the clans, mostly Macleans, Macleods, Camerons and the clan Chattan. Brushing aside Angus Mackay's small force of northern clans, he assembled his 10,000 men at Inverness and promised them the free plunder of Aberdeen.

Fortunately for Aberdeen, Alexander Stewart, Earl of Mar, a son of the Wolf of Badenoch and a relation of the Lord of the Isles, was as great and brave a warrior as Donald and had fought in Flanders. With the support of the burgesses of Aberdeen he collected an army and marched out to meet Donald. Though hopelessly outnumbered, Mar's army was superior in mail-clad knights and they held their own all afternoon and all night. By the morning the clans had vanished and only the dead remained. So many were slain in this action that it became known as 'Red Harlaw'.

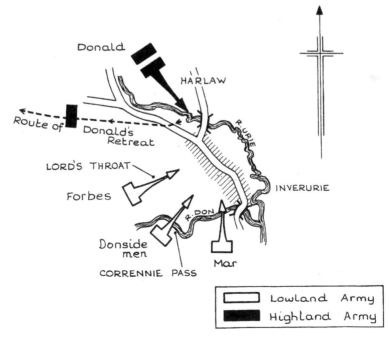

*Battle of Harlaw, 1411.*

Battle monument. (L. Potts)

Albany followed up the retreating Celts, capturing their stronghold at Dingwall. Donald finally submitted to Albany at Lochgilphead, Argyll. In 1424, after Albany's death, the rightful king of Scotland, James I, returned in triumph to rule his country with an English bride, Lady Jane Beaufort. The canny Scots carefully deducted £10,000 dowry from their £40,000 ransom before the agreement was signed – a piece of diplomacy that must have appealed to both Highlanders and Lowlanders alike.

## Harlaw Today

A few miles north of Inverurie there is a large monument commemorating the battle. It is found by turning off the B9001 after it crosses the little River Urie.

Robert Davidson, Provost of Aberdeen, was killed leading a group of citizens at Harlaw. He was buried by the north wall of St Nicholas' Church, Aberdeen, and the armour that can be seen in the entrance hall of Aberdeen's Town House is his, according to tradition.

# 13. (OLD) INVERLOCHY, 1 FEBRUARY 1645

## Lochaber, Highland OS 41 (121 755)

At Strathbogie, Hay and Sir James Drummond and many lowlanders left Montrose's army, probably due to the bloodshed after Aberdeen, but they wanted to make peace with Argyll. Montrose saw him as a chief enemy – he had confiscated his properties and had been responsible for imprisoning his chaplain, Wishart, and Lord Ogilvie

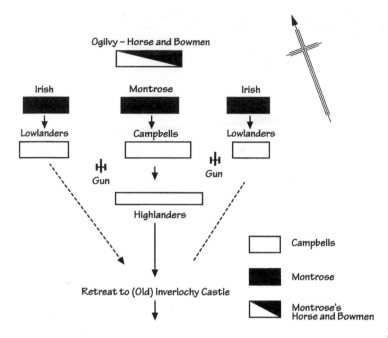

Battle of (Old) Inverlochy.

in Edinburgh Tollbooth. December in the Highlands was not a route to tarry and, guided by a Glencoe MacAlain, Montrose's army made for Inverary via Loch Tay and Glen Dochart. Argyll took to his boat on Loch Fyne as Montrose gathered up his army, which had had its full of Campbell cattle, to Connel (where there is still a ferry today) and with the help of Campbell of Ardchattan, who supplied boats in return for a promise not to have his property ruined, they all crossed safely and made for Lochaber. With the Earl of Seaforth and a mixed army of garrison men at Inverness and Argyll behind, it was no time to tarry and passing Inverlochy he made for Kilcummin (better known today as Fort Augustus) where his men signed a document to fight for King Charles I and against the 'desperate rebels now in fury against him'. Hugging the slopes of Ben Nevis, Montrose's little army returned to Inverlochy, now inhabited by Argyll's forces under Campbell of Auchinbreck – Argyll took to his boat again – but before the Campbells could eat their breakfast on Candlemas Day 1645, Montrose attacked, his Irish on each wing under Alasdair and O'Cahan and Montrose and the Highlanders in the centre. Ogilvy and some horse were behind. The Campbells alone stood their ground before being forced back on the second line where their forced allies, mostly Camerons, changed sides. The battle was soon over. Auchinbreck was killed and so too Lord Ogilvy. The number of Campbells slain almost equalled Montrose's army. The scene was set for the next battle: Auldearn, in May.

## Old Inverlochy Today

The old castle of Inverlochy must not be confused with the nineteenth-century castle built for Lord Abinger with its cherub ceiling in the hall. The old castle has been incorporated into a hotel. Pevsner calls it 'unloved'. The cairns that commemorate the battle are said to lose stones when a Campbell stops but gain stones when a Macdonald stops.

# 14. KILLIECRANKIE, 27 JULY 1689

Perth and Kinross OS Landranger 43 (905 639)

Despite his victory over the Duke of Monmouth at Sedgemoor, James VII (James II of England) was unable to retain his throne when in 1688 his son-in-law, William of Orange, was invited by Parliament to claim the crown on behalf of himself and his wife, Mary. James fled to France but, although the opposition to the newly crowned William III was negligible in England, in Scotland James' lieutenant was Viscount Dundee, an energetic and loyal soldier who had been Monmouth's second in command at Bothwell Bridge. Supported by the loyal Highland clans, Dundee made his base at Blair Atholl, where the Marquis of Atholl was waiting to see who would win the forthcoming encounter, for the Scottish Convention had, on William's orders, sent General Hugh Mackay and a strong body of regular troops to attack and defeat Dundee.

Arranging his army on the slopes of the hill behind and above Urrard House, Dundee waited for Mackay's soldiers to come out of Killiecrankie Pass on their way to Blair Castle. Dundee's men were not hidden, and Mackay must have realised that, although Dundee had a commanding position, his own forces were superior and his two troops of horse, placed in the centre, had some room to manoeuvre, while Dundee's few horsemen had a perilous hill to descend before they could come into action.

Killiecrankie pass. (Author)

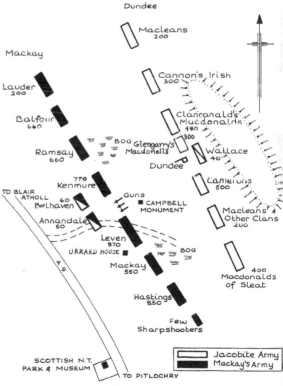

*Battle of Killiecrankie, 1689.*

Dundee arranged the Macleans on his right wing, then 300 Irish under Colonel Alexander Cannon, then Claranald's Macdonalds. On his left wing were the Macdonalds of Sleat, then a mixed group of clans, mostly Macleans, then Lochiel's Camerons, some of whom were sent down to occupy a cottage just above Urrard House. The few horse were commanded by Sir William Wallace, and Dundee, conspicuous in a silver and buff coat with a green scarf, placed himself in the centre; the standard of King James VII was carried by Alexander Macdonell of Glengarry. Facing him was Mackay's line of fusiliers and infantry under Lauder, Balfour, Ramsay, Kenmure, Leven and Hastings, with the cavalry in the centre under Belhaven and Annandale.

For two hours the two armies faced each other, Dundee waiting for the sun to move round until it was shining in the eyes of his enemy. Mackay's three guns were firing but seem to have done little damage. At 7.30 p.m. Dundee gave the signal to charge and, standing in his saddle to encourage his cavalry, was struck down in the opening minutes of the battle.

The Highlanders rushed forward, firing their muskets when within range, then discarding them and rushing on with dirks and claymores. The enemy reeled and gave way. Belhaven's and Annandale's cavalry, attacked by sixteen horsemen under the Earl of Dunfermline, retreated in disorder, and only Leven's regiment and part of that of Hastings remained on the scene with Mackay. Their accurate fire kept the clans at bay while they retreated, pursued by some of Wallace's horsemen, who had made a different descent from the hill to that made by Dunfermline.

Four hundred men, including Mackay, finally reached Stirling Castle, Dundee's body was taken to Old Blair where it lies buried in the churchyard. 1,000 of Mackay's men were killed and 500 taken prisoner. Two hundred Highlanders were killed by accurate infantry musketry, including Dundee. Colonel Cannon took over command of Dundee's army but failed to capture Dunkeld, which was stoutly held by Cleland's Cameronian regiment. The Jacobite victory at Killiecrankie was an isolated incident and one which did not stop Mackay from eventually subduing the Highlands.

## Killiecrankie Today

In 1964 the National Trust for Scotland in 1964 erected a small museum, which is now a visitor centre with information about the battle. This, with a large car park, stands on the A9 north of Pitlochry. The battle site, however, is further north on the lane leading to Orchilmore. The mound where the officers of both sides were buried is surmounted by a monument erected in 1950 to the memory of Ian Campbell Younger of Urrard, killed in Malaya at the age of twenty-four. It is a haunting spot, and the boggy ground and trees, if they were there in 1689, would have made cavalry action very difficult, which may explain why sixteen Jacobite horse made such an impression on Mackay's 110. There is a monument to Dundee in the ruined church at Old Blair. A recent archaeological dig has found a line of bullets further up the hill than where the battle was supposed to have taken place. This may be because some of Mackay's infantry had plug bayonets and wanted to fire their muskets before being in a position whereby they could only use their muskets for defence.

The visitors' centre has shop, café and car park. There are natural history walks (summer only). For details, telephone 01796 473233.

# 15. KILSYTH, 15 AUGUST 1645

North Lanarkshire OS Landranger 64 (741 787)

Auldearn and Alford confirmed the supremacy of the Marquis of Montrose's small army in the Highlands, but the south of Scotland still had to be captured from the hands of the Covenanters. In July William Baillie resigned from the governing Committee but was ordered to regain command of the new army which assembled at Perth on 24 July.

Montrose was strengthened by the return of Alexander Macdonald with 1,400 Irish and West Highlanders and by the arrival of Patrick Graham with the men of Atholl. He was now strong enough to threaten Perth but without cavalry he could not do more than this. Viscount Aboyne had been sent out again to find mounted reinforcements, having failed to produce any the first time. Eventually he arrived with 200 Gordon cavalry and some mounted musketeers.

Baillie caught some of the camp followers of Montrose's army in Methven Wood near Perth and slaughtered them. His forces now numbered 6,000 foot and 800 horse to Montrose's 4,500 foot and 500 horse. On 10 August Montrose went to Kinross and then turned on Castle Campbell at Dollar, which he burned. He then crossed the Forth at the Ford of Frew to get between Baillie, who had collected his Fife levies, and the new recruits from Glasgow under the Earl of Lanark. He found a commanding position at Kilsyth, where he waited for Baillie's army to catch up.

Baillie was hampered by his Committee, which had different views on how to fight Montrose. When a flank march to get round Montrose's army to the heights above him was proposed he was powerless to stop it. Some Covenanters under Major Haldane saw a few cottages occupied by the Macleans and, breaking their positions, they rushed on them. Macdonald, seeing the Macleans in action, broke out of line, charged the enemy and with the Macleans cut the Covenanters into two groups. The Gordon cavalry under Aboyne and his brother went to the height threatened by Baillie's horse and, when Aboyne was hard-pressed, the Ogilvies, commanded by their sixty-year-old chief, charged Lord Balcarres just as he was about to take the hill.

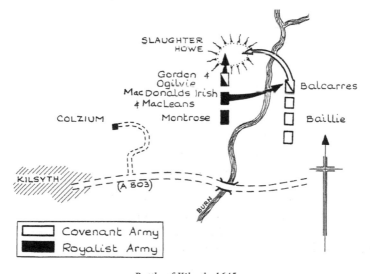

*Battle of Kilsyth, 1645.*

Kilsyth: the battle stone. (Author)

Baillie still had his Fife reserve and tried to hurry them to the rescue of his fast-dwindling army. They were not expert soldiers and many had fought at Tippermuir the year before, when they had Montrose's army at its fiercest. They turned and fled.

The Fife men were cut down in their hundreds, for the Highlanders were out to revenge the slaughter of their womenfolk in Methven Wood. Barely 100 of the foot escaped. The cavalry were more fortunate: some escaped by ship to Berwick-upon-Tweed; others went to Stirling or Carlisle.

## Kilsyth Today

The battlefield of Kilsyth is mostly covered by a reservoir. The local topography is, or was, called by bloodthirsty names like Slaughter Howe, Drum Burn and Kill-the-Many Butts. The manor of Colzium, which lies off the A803 a mile (1.6 km) before Kilsyth when coming from Stirling, is now Colzium Margaret Lennox Memorial Estate, administered by North Lanarkshire District Council. A round stone battle monument in the grounds is inscribed around its rim, 'The Marquis of Montrose won his greatest and last victory near Colzium.' In the Argyll and Sutherland Highlander's Regimental Museum in Stirling Castle is a silver relief of the battle on a statue of Montrose on horseback.

# 16. LANGSIDE, 13 MAY 1568

## Glasgow OS Landranger 64 (581 615)

On the death of her husband, the French Dauphin, Mary returned to Scotland as queen. In 1565 she married Lord Darnley, but two years later he was murdered, and Mary was suspected of complicity in the crime. She was imprisoned at Lochleven by the Regent Moray (her half-brother) and his confederates, but escaped. Making for Dumbarton with her supporters, Mary collected a force of 5,000 under Argyll and the Hamiltons. Nearly 100 barons, nine earls, nine bishops, eighteen lords and twelve abbots and priors signed a pledge to defend Mary and restore her to her throne.

Moray was an astute leader, and his small force occupied Langside Hill, which is today in Queen's Park, Glasgow. Sir William Kirkcaldy of Grange commanded

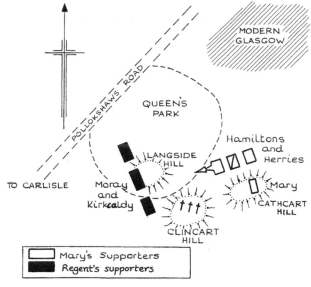

*Battle of Langside, 1568.*

200 picked musketeers in Langside village. They were mounted behind horsemen for manoeuvrability, and on the left wing Moray's infantry occupied Pathead Farm. The Hamiltons attempted to seize the village and Lord Herries led two cavalry charges against Kirkcaldy. Moray's cavalry fought them off, and the Hamiltons, bypassing Clincart Hill where Moray had stationed his guns, climbed the hill to the village where they were set upon by the musketeers. The spears were levelled, and in the cramped site many men, especially the queen's main force, were trampled by the fleeing Hamiltons. Kirkcaldy now led the reserve down on the flank and front of the queen's centre, and only the cavalry of Lord Herries saved Mary, who had been watching the battle from Cathcart, and enabled her to escape to Dumfries and across the Solway Firth to Workington. Queen Elizabeth I of England took her chance and Mary was never again a free agent. Langside was one of the most decisive battles fought on Scottish soil.

## Langside Today

The tall granite monument to the battle lies at the south side of Queen's Park, which can be reached from Central Station down Eglinton Street and Pollokshaws Road to Langside Avenue, which leads left to the monument, topped by a lion, on a traffic island.

# 17. PHILIPHAUGH, 13 SEPTEMBER 1645

## Scottish Borders OS Landranger 73 (445 282)

After Kilsyth the Marquis of Montrose occupied Glasgow, but instead of gaining support his army disintegrated. Alexander Macdonald and half the Irish troops left for Galloway and Viscount Aboyne returned to the north with the Gordons.

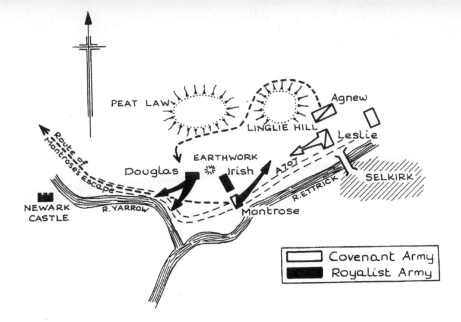

*Battle of Philiphaugh, 1645.*

With scarcely 700 men, Montrose set out for the borders, as instructed by Charles I, hoping to pick up recruits on the way, especially from the earls of Home and Roxburgh. But he was to be disappointed, and in England General David Leslie, who had been besieging Hereford, moved north with around 6,000 men, most of whom were mounted.

Advised by Lord Erskine to retreat, Montrose was determined to find allies, but when he reached Kelso no one came forward and at Jedburgh the local laird was a Covenanter general. On 12 September the small Royalist force reached the junction of the Yarrow and Ettrick rivers. Montrose camped here with the rivers protecting two flanks, a steep hill to the north and only the track from Selkirk providing any easy access. During the night Lord Linton, the son of the Earl of Traquair, withdrew and, according to tradition, went to Leslie in his camp, which was between Galashiels and Selkirk, probably at Sunderland Hall, where he drove out some Royalists.

Early next morning Leslie was on the move. He divided his army into two groups, one of which consisted of 2,000 dragoons and was commanded by Agnew of Lochnaw. Guided by a local man, they went around Linglie Hill and advanced on Montrose's rear. The other group under Leslie moved down the riverbank towards Philiphaugh. It was a misty day and Montrose, with a few horsemen, was at a house in West Port in Selkirk when he was roused by his scoutmaster, who told him the news. The sudden emergence from the mist of Leslie's cavalry on the Irish was a shock. They had built some shallow trenches, but the Marquis of Douglas's men fled at once and the Irish were soon hopelessly outnumbered when Agnew's men burst down on their rear.

Montrose, collecting a small force of cavalry, crossed the Ettrick, joined his army, which was already under attack, and attempted to hold up Leslie's horse. His few cavalry fought bravely but, soon realising that all was lost, they fled over Minch Moor to Traquair House, where they were refused admission. The Irish under their adjutant Stewart surrendered and were slaughtered on their march to captivity, along with their womenfolk, who were mostly shot in the courtyard of nearby Newark Castle. Montrose and around thirty followers reached the safety of the Highlands, but his year of victories was over.

*Left*: Montrose's effigy in St Giles Cathedral, Edinburgh. (ARN Kinross).
*Right*: Newark Castle. (Author)

## Philiphaugh Today

The battlefield stands in private land in the grounds of Philiphaugh House, just off the A708 and around 2 miles (3 km) west of Selkirk. There is a monument to the memory of 'the Covenanters who fought and gained the battle'. The field opposite is called Battlefield and there are traces of an earthwork at one end. Permission should be obtained to see the monument. Newark Castle is further west along the A708, across the Yarrow, and can be glimpsed through the trees close to the inscribed remains of the birthplace of the explorer Mungo Park.

# 18. PINKIE, 10 SEPTEMBER 1547

## East Lothian OS Landranger 66 (361 716)

In 1547 Henry VIII died and it was again suggested that his young son, now King Edward VI, should marry the four-year-old Mary, Queen of Scots. The Duke of Somerset, ruler of England during Edward's minority, was determined to teach the Scots a lesson. They were seeking aid from Henry II of France, and Somerset, a man who saw everything in terms of black or white, decided that either they must agree to the wedding and break up their French alliance or he would declare war. The Earl of Arran, who was Regent of Scotland, had a considerable army, some of which had taken part in the siege of St Andrews, which had been held by heretics for over a month and was finally captured in July 1547 with the help of a French fleet.

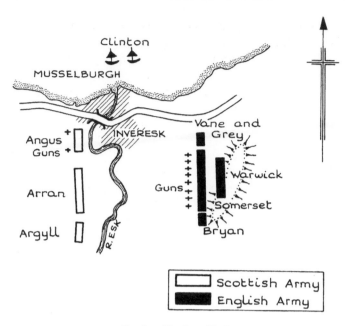

*Battle of Pinkie, 1547.*

The English army of nearly 18,000 was at Newcastle upon Tyne at the end of August. It was very well organised by Somerset and included fifteen pieces of artillery, 2,000 light horse under Sir Frances Bryan, 4,000 cavalry under Vane and Lord Grey de Wilton and 600 hackbuteers under St Peter Mewtus. There was a mounted division similarly equipped under Gamboa, a Spaniard, whose men were the first to use firearms, at the siege of Rhey in 1521. Lord Clinton's fleet accompanied the English army. It consisted of thirty warships and the same number of transports. No army had entered Scotland as well equipped; they even had pioneers to clear the route for their wagons.

Arran, no soldier but a shrewd politician, had arranged his army, which exceeded the English by several thousand – some accounts say it was as many as 34,000 – along the River Esk. The solitary bridge was barricaded and protected by artillery and the sea flank by a raised entrenchment and more artillery. The Earl of Angus, with his spearmen, formed the left flank, Arran and the men of Stirling, Edinburgh and the Lowlands the centre, and on the right wing were Highlanders under Argyll.

On 9 September the heavily armed English cavalry fought off Lord Home's lightly armed horsemen. The next morning, Somerset, having refused an offer of single combat from the Scottish Earl of Huntly, decided to put his artillery on Fawside Hill so that it would command the Scottish position. At this stage Arran took his forces across the river to confront the English army. In response, Lord Grey led his cavalry forward, followed by the infantry, and found the Scottish spearmen arranged in squares, the first ranks kneeling, the second sloping forward and the third rank standing – it was like charging a hedgehog. The muddy ground unhorsed many of the cavalry. Grey was wounded and around 200 of his men were killed. Warwick, in command of the second line, rushed forward with Mewtus's hackbuteers and Gamboa's horsemen. The combined fire and that of the English guns successfully broke the squares and the left wing disintegrated.

Arran, who had held such a fine position, had sacrificed it by trying to cut off the English from their ships. The guns of Clinton's ships in Musselburgh played a decisive part. One lucky shot is supposed to have killed the Master of Graham and twenty-five horsemen. Presumably the Esk was wider and deeper in those days, and it is possible that the ships came up the river. The slaughter was frightful: a regiment of monks from Dunfermline was cut down to a man. The Earl of Huntly was captured and Arran retreated to Stirling.

Somerset burnt Leith and after a week retreated to England as his army was short of food. The Scottish alliance with France was strengthened and 6,000 French soldiers arrived under Sieur d'Esse, a dashing commander in battle but quarrelsome when not. Mary was sent to France, where she married the young Dauphin François. In 1550 by the Treaty of Boulogne, the English had to give up their French possessions, and in Scotland the town of Haddington, fortified by Lord Grey after Pinkie, had already been abandoned because of plague. It was a hollow victory, and the English campaign of 1547 came to be known by the Scots as 'the rough wooing'.

After his success at Pinkie, Somerset had the following letter from his godson, the sixteen-year-old King Edward VI:

Dearest Uncle,

By your letters and report of the messenger, we have a good length understanded to our great comfort, the good success, it hathe pleased god to gain us against the Scottes by your good courage and wise forsight, for the which and other the benefites of god heaped upon us, like as we are most bounden to yield him most humble thanks, and to seke by as waies we may his true honesty, so do we give unto you, good uncle our most hastie thanks, praying you to thanke also most handie in our name, our good cosin th'Erle of Warwike, and all the others of the noble men, our gentlemen, and others that have served in this journey, of whose servise they shall be well assured, we will not (god gararunte us life) shew ourselves unmindfull, but be ready ever to consider the same as at this occasion shall serve.

Ye are at our house of Orlandes, the eighteenth of September.

Your good nephew,

Edward

Not many sixteen-year-olds today could write such a letter, and the young king was obviously aware of his illness ('god guarantee us life') for he dies six years later before history can make up its mind whether or not he would have been a great king.

## Pinkie Today

Known as 'Pinkie Cleugh' in Scotland – 'Cleugh' meaning a gully or cutting – the battlefield of Pinkie is best explored on foot from Inveresk. The ridge held by the English is clearly visible and the actual battle must have covered a large area. It is hard to imagine the English fleet being able to come in close enough to train its cannon on the Scots. Pinkie House in Musselburgh is named after the battle but otherwise has no connection. Musselburgh Bridge is there, though used by pedestrians only. Inveresk Bridge has a small monument and in Bunbury, Cheshire, there is a monument to Sir George Beeston, who died at the age of 102 'and fought gallantly contra Scots apud Musselburgh'.

# 19. PRESTONPANS, 21 SEPTEMBER 1745

## East Lothian OS Ranger 66 (402 742)

Prince Charles Edward Stuart, son of James, the Old Pretender, landed on the west coast of Scotland in July 1745, accompanied by nine men and a few arms, to claim the throne from George II. England was at war with France, and a planned French invasion in 1744 had been destroyed by a gale. Support for Charles was slow at first but, with the arrival of the Clan Cameron, other clans began to rally to the Prince's standard, which was raised at Glenfinnan on 19 August.

Prince Charles' Highland army marched into Edinburgh at noon on 17 September 1745, having captured it during the night without any resistance. Only the castle remained in government hands. Near Dunbar, however, was Lieutenant General Sir John Cope with six squadrons of dragoons, three companies of foot and some Scottish volunteers. The Highlanders had few arms and no mobile artillery; their cavalry was around forty men and their main force numbered 2,400. Cope's army numbered 3,000 and included artillery manned by naval gunners.

The Scots were armed with broad sword, dirk and targe (a small circular shield), and some had pistols. Very few had 'muskets, fuses or fowling pieces'. They were fast-moving and fierce when they charged. The English redcoats had muskets with bayonets. These needed ramrods for loading and the cartridge had to be bitten to sprinkle power into the firing pan; as a result, they were too slow to reload at Prestonpans and the weather was

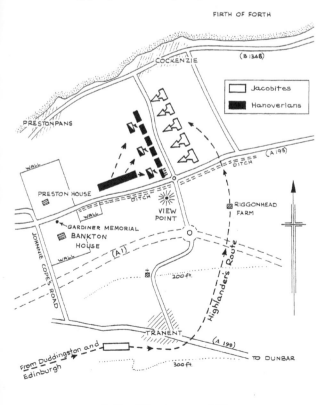

*Battle of Prestonpans, 1745.*

against them at Falkirk. It was only at Culloden that the English infantrymen, firing in three ranks, one rank at a time, and then thrusting their bayonets at the unguarded side of the Highlanders, were effective.

On 19 September Princes Charles held a council of war at Duddingston where his Highlanders were camping. Next day they moved out towards Musselburgh. Cope moved more slowly to Haddington and took up a position on 20 September near Preston House, less than a mile from the sea, with a cornfield in which his dragoons could manoeuvre and the marshy Tranent meadows protecting his south flank. Lord George Murray, in command of the Highland vanguard, immediately positioned the prince's army on Falside Hill near Tranent, where he could observe the government army without difficulty.

The strength of Cope's position was soon apparent to Murray, who realised that the Tranent meadows were poor ground for charging Highlanders, for as well as being very marshy in places they were crossed by dry stone dykes. A local man, Anderson, suggested a hidden path to the west of Rigganhead farm that could bring the Highland army round to Cope's weakest flank, the east. Setting off at 4.00 a.m. on Saturday 21 September, they had reached the farm when a shot rang out.

One of Cope's patrols had spotted them. The government army was hastily repositioned facing east with the guns on the right wing and three dragoon squadrons in the second line. Next to the guns were Colonel James Gardiner's dragoons. The colonel, no longer a fit man, had played a large part in the victory at Preston over the Jacobites in 1715.

The Camerons on the Highland left charged as soon as the last of the rearguard had arrived on the field. With few shots from their guns and mortars taking effect, the government gunners fled, the dragoons and artillery regiment following them. With the sun in their eyes and the long line of advancing Highlanders in front, the government army thought they were outnumbered. The dragoons on the left wing rode off towards Prestonpans and Cope himself, having tried to rally his men, led a party of 400 stragglers up a side road (now known as Johnnie Cope's Road) to the Highlanders' first position. They did not stop until they reached the safety of Berwick-upon-Tweed. Colonel Gardiner, whose home, Bankton House, was beside the battlefield, was mortally wounded by an axe and died the following day in the manse at Tranent. He was buried in Tranent churchyard. Some 500 government infantry and dragoons were killed, 1,400 were captured and many wounded. The Highlanders lost thirty, killed, and seventy were wounded, and on their march into England that followed, the ballad 'Hey Johnnie Cope are ye walking yet?' was sung by the conquerors as a marching song.

*Opposite, right*: The battle cairn. (Author)

*Right*: The battlefield viewpoint. (Author)

## Prestonpans Today

Take the A1(T) from Edinburgh towards Berwick and turn left for Cockenzie. The area through which the Highlanders marched was later an open-cast coal mine but much of it has now been reinstated. At Meadowmill roundabout turn left, and at a battle cairn on the left follow signs to the battleside viewpoint on top of a former slag heap. Interpretation panels tell the story with clear diagrams.

Further along the road from Meadowmill viewpoint, before the railway station, the monument to Colonel Gardiner can be seen across the railway line in the grounds of Bankton House.

There is a large car park at East Lothian Bowling Club with a footpath to the visitor viewpoint on the coal-spoil heap. Apart from Colonel Gardiner's monument, there is one in Preston churchyard to Colonel Stuart of Phisgul, 'Barbarously murdered by four highlanders near the end of the Battle.'

Bonny Prince Charlie would not recognise this place now as there is so much development, main roads and railway whereas in 1745 there were salt pans and a small coal mine with a wagon way to the sea, marked on the description panels.

# 20. SHERIFFMUIR, 13 NOVEMBER 1715

## Stirling OS Landranger 57 (822 017)

On 6 September 1715 the Jacobite standard of James VIII was raised at Braemar by the Earl of Mar, who had been dismissed by George I from his post as Secretary of State for Scotland. With a commission from James VIII and the promise of help from France, the 1715 rebellion

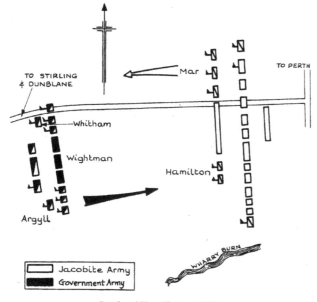

*Battle of Sheriffmuir, 1715.*

started with a far better chance of success than its successor thirty years later. The Protestant loyalists rallied at Stirling, the local militias commanded by General Joseph Wightman and under overall command of the Duke of Argyll, a capable soldier and statesman.

Mar dallied at Perth while the clans came in slowly. On 10 November he left with nearly 10,000 men and joined General Gordon at Auchterarder. Plans were made to approach the Forth in four divisions and to avoid Stirling, where Argyll's force numbered only 3,000 men. Argyll's spies brought word that Gordon's men were approaching Dunblane, and on Sunday 12 November he moved first, occupied the town and camped his army 2 miles (3 km) north-east above Kippenross House. He knew the area well because the local militia used Sheriffmuir as a training ground.

Mar was annoyed that Gordon had been unable to take Dunblane, and on the approach of darkness he ordered his men to camp at Kinbuck. 'It cannot be said we had a front or rear any more than has a barrel of herrings' was the comment of the Master of Sinclair. Early next morning Mar drew up his forces at the eastern end of Sheriffmuir, his left wing protected by a bog. Argyll drew up his army, which, though small in number, was superior in cavalry. The burns had frozen over in the night, so he had chosen his position from a cavalry commander's point of view. Argyll scouted out the Jacobite's position from his right wing (he stood where the Gathering Stone can still be seen) and ordered his drums to beat the advance.

When the two armies came in sight of each other, the right wings of both sides' front ranks outflanked the opposition. Mar quickly ordered the Macleans to charge; the Duke of Argyll, spotting the Jacobite left wing out of line as it circled a bog, brought up his heavy cavalry, and only a gallant stand by the Fife and Angus horse prevented the complete collapse of Mar's left wing. Meanwhile Argyll's left wing collapsed and General Whitham fled back to Stirling. From Argyll's right the Scots Greys and Evans' dragoons slaughtered the light horsemen opposite them, while the Macraes in Seaforth's battalions were killed almost to a man.

When Argyll returned with around 1,000 men he found that he was outnumbered, so he ordered Wightman to take up a defensive position with his cannon. Seeing what had happened to his other wing, the Earl of Mar retreated, losing four cannon, thirteen colours and nearly 800 killed or captured. On the other hand he had captured four colours and 1,400 arms; Argyll had lost 290 killed and over 100 taken prisoner.

The rising soon collapsed, partly due to the capture by Argyll of so many Highland leaders and the desertion of the clans at Perth. When James finally arrived, it was too late to raise an army again. Mar fled to France, where he died in 1732.

The surprising feature of the battle is the behaviour of both commanders in charging with their wings and ignoring the rest of their armies. Mar did send a messenger to

Sheriffmuir: the
Gathering Stone. (Author)

General Hamilton, who commanded his left, but according to one account the messenger was a traitor and delayed his message until it was too late. The ground is hilly in the middle, like a large-scale camber, and it is possible that Argyll saw only the wing he attacked, but this does not explain the conduct of his centre troops. Mar's centre fought with his right and in both armies artillery appears to have played no significant part.

## Sheriffmuir Today

Around 2 miles north-east of Dunblane, the battlefield is marked by a large monument to the Macraes, killed almost to a man as they were stationed on the left wing. The gathering stone, where the clans sharpened their dirks, is now on the end of a muddy footpath and has iron hoops over it to stop souvenir hunters. The crystal stone, the *Clach na Brattich*, used by the Robertsons at this battle and at Culloden, can be seen at their museum near Blair Atholl. Burns speaks of 'Crowdie time' and at the time of this battle Crowdie cheese was popular with the Highlanders:

> My sister Kate came up the gate
> Wi' crowdie unto me man
> She swore she saw the rebels ran
> Frae Perth under Dundee man.

We don't know what happened to Kate's brother, but he was well looked after, you can be sure.

Macrae monument. (ARN Kinross)

# 21. STIRLING BRIDGE, 11 SEPTEMBER 1297

Stirling OS Landranger 57 (784 950)

The death of Alexander III, king of Scots, in 1286 left the Scottish succession in doubt. There were two main contenders for the throne: Robert Bruce and John Balliol, his cousin. In England Edward I naturally preferred the weaker man, and in 1292 Balliol was declared king. He promptly did homage to Edward, who became ruler in all but name. When Scotland was asked to supply troops to defend Gascony, Balliol objected and in 1295 he signed a peace treaty with the French court.

In 1296 Balliol surrendered Scotland to Edward without the acquiescence of the Scots. The Earl of Surrey was appointed governor of the country or, in reality, of the English garrisons, and his treasurer was Hugh Cressingham. In times of crises Scotland always seemed to produce the right leader and in 1297 William Wallace, the second son of a little-known knight from Paisley who had been killed by the English, emerged as the leading patriot. He gathered an army with his friends Moray, Ramsay and Graham and besieged Dundee, which was in English hands. Cressingham and Surrey made for Stirling with a large army – 50,000 men according to some reports – but it was probably less than half that number, although it certainly outnumbered Wallace's.

Wallace doubled back at great speed from Dundee to hold the Forth crossing. The river was spanned by a single wooden bridge 1 mile (1.6 km) upstream from the place

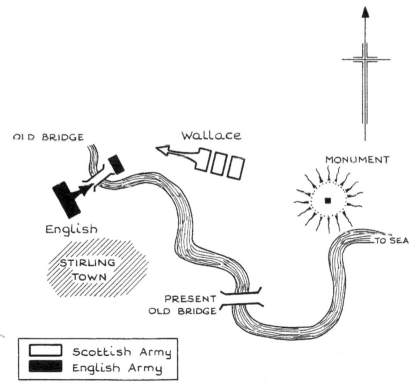

*Battle of Stirling Bridge, 1297.*

Stirling Bridge and on the horizon, the Wallace Monument. (ARN Kinross)

where the old stone bridge stands today. The Scottish carpenters fixed the bridge so that it could be demolished by the quick removal of a single timber. Wright, in charge, was nicknamed 'Pin' Wright, and so too the firstborn boy of all the Wright family since.

Wallace then camped on Abbey Craig Hill and awaited developments. Two Dominican friars were sent to Wallace by Surrey to make peace, but this was firmly refused. A Scottish knight in Edward's army – he had many Balliol supporters of doubtful reliability – volunteered to take some horse over the river by a nearby ford. Cressingham urged a simple crossing of the wooden bridge and, afraid of being superseded as governor, Surrey agreed. A party of Scots attacked from Cambuskenneth Abbey and held the Scottish side of the bridge. The English vanguard under Sir Marmaduke de Twenge charged the Scots as they descended, but the Scottish archers caused havoc in the dense English ranks. Some reinforcements got across before the bridge collapsed, and Sir Marmaduke was one of the few to escape, with some of his cavalry.

Meanwhile the Scottish horse, around 200 in number, had crossed by the ford and harried the English retreat. The English were driven to Berwick. Thousands were killed, including Cressingham. Edward was forced to give up his plan, but the following year he returned with a larger army and defeated Wallace at Falkirk.

## Stirling Bridge Today

The old bridge at Stirling today next to the modern one dates from 1400 and is around 1 mile (1.6 km) downstream from where the battle is supposed to have taken place. A visit to the Wallace Monument to see the excellent audio-visual displays and the lie of the land is recommended. The site is a half-hour walk from Bannockburn on a nice day.

# 22. TIPPERMUIR, 1 SEPTEMBER 1644

OS Landranger 58 (238 061)

James Graham, Marquis of Montrose, appears at this time in Scotland as Lieutenant General of King Charles' forces in Scotland. He had no army until he was joined by Alasdair MacDonald and his Irish at Blair Atholl, his headquarters. Some Highlanders came in plus Kilpont and 500 bowmen. He had no artillery and his few Irish with guns had only one round each. Against him at Tippermuir near Perth was Lord Elcho and a Covenanting army of 7,700, of whom 700 were horsemen under Lord Drummond, who were mainly local gentry. In charge was Lord Elcho, whose relation was one of Prince Charles' cavalry leaders 100 years later.

The battle at Tippermuir outside Perth started with a move forward by Drummond's horse. They were greeted by a volley by the Irish, some of whom had to throw stones. The Covenant centre gave way and men flew into Perth. The Irish followed and Montrose had to discipline them from sacking the city. The tents, drums, baggage and guns of the enemy were scooped up and for three days the army remained in Perth, fining the burghers £50, which went to new uniforms for the Irish. Argyll and a force of Campbells were approaching from the west so on 4 September Montrose left Perth to get more men in his own territory of Angus across the River Tay. Tippermuir had been a start. The road map calls it Tibbermore today.

Montrose's route to Tippermuir.

# NORTHERN ENGLAND & MIDLANDS

## 23. ADWALTON MOOR, 30 JUNE 1643

West Yorkshire OS Landranger 104 (222 283)

In 1643 the Civil War in Yorkshire developed into a struggle between the Parliamentarian Baron Fairfax and his son, Sir Thomas Fairfax, who held Leeds, Bradford and the recently captured Wakefield, and the Earl of Newcastle's Royalists, who had been strengthened by the arrival earlier in the year of fresh armaments from abroad when Queen Henrietta Maria's ships put into Bridlington.

At the end of June Newcastle set out with nearly 10,000 men to storm Howley House, home of the Parliamentarian Lord Savile near Pontefract. He then moved on Bradford, determined to secure the West Riding of Yorkshire for the king and to forge a safe passage for the queen's small army to get through to Oxford.

On 30 June Sir Thomas Fairfax's cavalry and his father's infantry moved out of Bradford, which was ill provisioned for a siege, and took up a position on Adwalton Moor, blocking the approach road from Leeds. In number they were around 5,000 but, apart from the local clubmen, they were better armed than the Royalists. Newcastle had

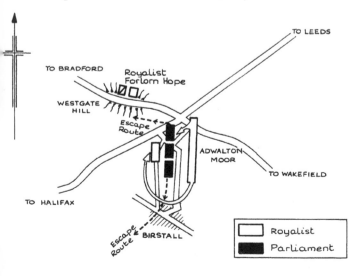

*Battle of Adwalton Moor, 1643.*

Earl of Newcastle. (Grant)

with him two heavy guns, *Gog* and *Magog*, and he spread his large army out on the moor so that it outflanked the hard-pressed Parliamentary forces. The Forlorn Hope, consisting of dragoons, horse and foot raised in Northumberland at the expense of Sir Robert Clavering of Callaly Castle, who commanded it, was positioned on Westgate Hill. The Fairfaxes held their ground, but the left flank of infantry under Major-General John Gifford was charged by a regiment of pikemen under Colonel Heron, of Newcastle's famous Whitecoats regiment. It faltered and gave way. At the same time a troop of Royalist horse made their way round to the rear of Fairfax's centre. The luckless Sir Thomas fled to Halifax and the remains of Gifford's and Lord Fairfax's men retreated to Bradford, where they were attacked the following day. The Royalists lost a few men including Colonel Heron, whose body was stripped by four Roundheads who, Lord Fairfax noted, were all killed by a single shot from one of the Royalist guns shortly after their misdeed. The Roundheads lost 500 men killed, 1,400 taken prisoner and three guns.

After forty hours in the saddle Lord Fairfax reached Hull, but his son, whose wife was captured by Newcastle, lost most of his men in his escape when they were intercepted at Selby. Newcastle charitably sent Lady Fairfax in his own coach to her husband. The queen, with 3,000 infantry and thirty troops of horse, rode into Oxford, and the Royalists, after unsuccessfully besieging Hull, retreated to York, where the following year 'Black' Tom Fairfax joined with Cromwell and had his revenge at Marston Moor.

## Adwalton Moor Today

The moor is a large green at the junction of the A50 and A282. The area is industrial, but the lane from Oakwell to Cleckheaton and Halifax, which was taken by Sir Thomas Fairfax in his retreat, still exists and it was probably the top part of this route which was used by Newcastle to send his attacking force to strike Lord Fairfax in the rear. Clavering's regiment was presumably stationed on Westgate Hill to cut off the retreat to Bradford, which they failed to do, although Lord Fairfax and Gifford may have used a different route in their escape. There is a battle stone with plaque at Drighlington on the A650 out of Bradford.

# 24. BLORE HEATH, 23 SEPTEMBER 1459

## Staffordshire OS Landranger 127 (713 352)

The first battle of St Albans in 1455 ended with an uneasy four-year truce. By 1459 the Duke of York was apprehensive about Queen Margaret's behaviour. She monopolised the King's Council with her favourite, the Earl of Wiltshire, and in Cheshire she was distributing the badge of the swan – the sign of the Prince of Wales, her son – to men who joined the Lancastrian army. York set out for Wales to raise an army, and Lord Salisbury, father of the Earl of Warwick, who was in Calais, went to Middleham in Yorkshire to equip his faithful Yorkists and then set out for Ludlow with 5,000 men.

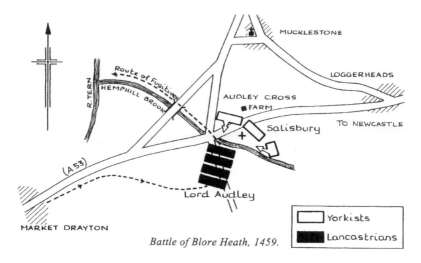

*Battle of Blore Heath, 1459.*

☐ Yorkists
■ Lancastrians

The plan was to unite the two Yorkist armies at Ludlow Castle and march on London. Queen Margaret was well informed. She and Henry were in Nottingham in September but moved to Eccleshall with the large Lancastrian army. She detached Lord Audley with nearly 10,000 men to arrest Salisbury and he blocked Salisbury's way outside Market Drayton. The wily Salisbury suspected the move or, more probably, his spies told him the position of the Lancastrians, for he moved off the Newcastle-under-Lyme road and took up a position overlooking Hemphill Brook. He carefully concealed the two wings of his army behind the slope so that Lord Audley, advancing, saw only the central body and promptly attacked on a narrow front. Salisbury made a feint retreat and then brought up his wings when Audley's heavily mounted knights were crossing the steep-sided brook. Twice the Lancastrians tried to charge but the spears and bills of the Yorkists beat them back. During Audley's third charge, this time by infantry, the Cheshire archers were too hemmed in to use their bows and so were easy targets for the Yorkist archers. Audley was killed and his army broke. Many fled along the stream bed to where it joins the River Tern and were killed in the stampede to get across.

Blore Heath: the memorial cross, as repaired in 1765. (Postcard)

The 2,000 Lancastrian dead included Sir Thomas Dutton, Sir Hugh Venables and Sir John Leigh. Salisbury had won one of the most overwhelming victories in the Wars of the Roses but it was not followed through. Salisbury joined up with Richard, Duke of York, and with Warwick at Ludlow but, faced with the king's superior army, the Yorkist leaders fled abroad and their army surrendered at Ludford Bridge.

## Blore Heath Today

The battlefield lies across the main A53 road from Market Drayton to Newcastle-under-Lyme. To find the memorial cross, which is in the field opposite Audley Cross Farm, stop by the crossroads around 4 miles (6.5 km) from Market Drayton. Park in one of the side roads. The cross is in the field on the other side of the brook and can just be seen from the A53 when there are no crops. The road to the left goes to the village of Mucklestone, where there is a plaque on a cottage that faces an inscribed anvil in the churchyard. This states that Queen Margaret, having seen from the church tower that her army had lost, fled with the shoes on her horse hastily reversed by Shufnall, the local smith, whose descendants have a gravestone in the churchyard. How she found herself behind enemy lines is not clear, and the legend is improbable.

# 25. BOROUGHBRIDGE, 16 MARCH 1322

North Yorkshire OS Landranger 99 (394 671)

Battle of Boroughbridge plaque on the bridge. (ARN Kinross)

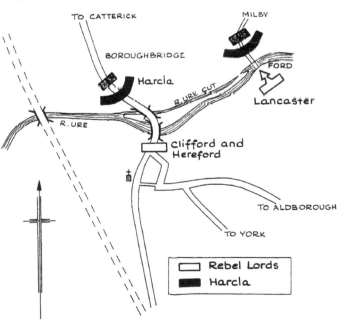

*Battle of Boroughbridge, 1322.*

After Bannockburn the English crown was constantly threatened not only by the Scots but also by the rebellious barons. Edward II's favourite, Piers Gaveston, was captured by Guy de Beauchamp, Earl of Warwick, and Thomas, Earl of Lancaster, but the king found new favourites in Hugh le Despenser and his son, and they were soon as unpopular in the Welsh Marches as Gaveston had been in the country as a whole. At the Parliament that met in 1321 the two Despensers were banished and the barons pardoned themselves for acting against the favourites. Edward now looked for any chance to get his revenge. When the queen was refused admission to Leeds Castle in Kent, he collected an army of Londoners and attacked the castle, which held out for two weeks. When it fell he imprisoned Lady Badlesmere, the owner, and hanged the garrison.

Civil war broke out and Edward marched on Bridgnorth, where Mortimer was gathering an army of rebels. Mortimer was soon defeated and Lancaster, who had raised a strong force in Yorkshire that included the rebel lords Mowbray, Clifford, Amory and Hereford, set out to Tickhill, near Doncaster, where he besieged the royal castle. The garrison held out and, as the king's troops advanced from Cirencester, Lancaster checked them at Burton-on-Trent, but Edward crossed the river higher up and pursued the rebels back to Yorkshire. The vanguard of the Earls of Surrey and Kent captured the rebel held castles of Tutbury and Kenilworth. Lancaster's only hope was to join forces with the Scots, and on 16 March 1322, his army reached the River Ure at Boroughbridge.

Meanwhile Sir Andrew Harcla, Edward's warden of Carlisle, had come south with his spearmen and archers. Hearing from a spy that the rebels were making for Boroughbridge, he placed his army in two schiltrons on the north bank, putting archers behind the spearman so that one group could fire easily at the bridge and the other could defend the nearby Milby ford. Lancaster, who had no quarrel with Harcla, tried to reason with him and, when this failed, exclaimed that the knight 'would sorely repent and should die a shameful death ere another year should expire'.

Lancaster led his horsemen at the ford while Clifford and Hereford dismounted and attacked the bridge. The struggle was fierce. Perhaps remembering Stamford Bridge, one of the Welsh spearmen killed Hereford by thrusting at him from under the bridge. Clifford was wounded and Lancaster could not force the ford. Calling off the remainder of his men, many of whom had deserted, he made a truce with Harcla and camped in the town for the night. Next day Sir Simon de Ward brought 500 men to assist Harcla,

The bridge today at Boroughbridge. (Author).

Battle monument at Aldborough. (Author)

and Lancaster, with a few remaining followers, was forced into the church. Many of the knights escaped dressed as peasants but Lancaster was captured and led to his own castle of Pontefract. There King Edward and Hugh de Despenser held a mock trial and, 'riding a sorry nag', the 'mightiest earl in Christendom' was led out to his execution.

In October 1322 Robert the Bruce attacked Edward's army at Byland in Yorkshire and routed them. Harcla made his own peace and the Earl of Lancaster's prophesy came true. The victor at Boroughbridge was accused of treachery, tried, hanged drawn and quartered.

## Boroughbridge Today

The town is 20 miles (32 km) north-west of York on the A1. The river is around 20 feet (6 metres) wide and suffers from frequent winter floods. There is a riverside walk to Milby Lock which passes the ford, but the river must have been shallower in 1322. A monument to the battle formerly stood in the main street but was moved some years ago to the neighbouring village of Aldborough. There is a small blue circle on the town end of the bridge commemorating the battle.

# 26. BOSWORTH FIELD, 22 AUGUST 1485

## Leicestershire OS Landranger 140 (405 005)

The Battle of Bosworth is one of the most important of all English battles as it changed the dynasty of England and led to the birth of the Tudors. Many men sat 'on the fence' until the outcome was known. Only the Duke of Norfolk, leading Richard's vanguard,

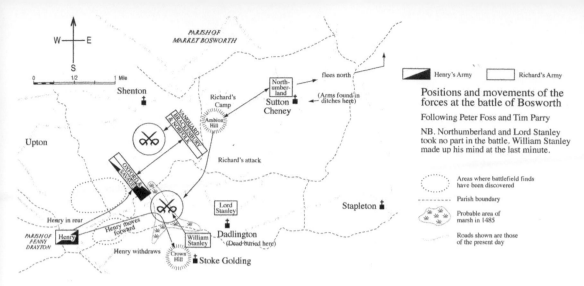

Battle of Bosworth 1485.

fought Henry's vanguard under Lord Oxford. Norfolk was strengthened by the king's artillery, mostly small handheld guns but one or two of larger calibre as metal detectors have found cannonballs in 'Redesmere', a boggy area near to where William Stanley was camped. His brother, Lord Stanley's 3,500 troops stood on a hill outside Dudlington (where bodies were buried later in the churchyard) and, as his son Lord Strange was a hostage in Richard's hands, did nothing at all during the battle but watch.

With Northumberland in the rear, Richard's forces were nearly 10,000 to Henry's 5,000, which didn't count the 5,500 Stanleys looking on. Oxford formed his men into a wedge and, when Norfolk was killed they moved slowly forward towards Ambion Hill.

Impatient Richard spotted Henry's banners moving forward towards the marshy area of Redesmere (sometimes called Red Mere). He cut down the Tudor's standard bearer and, at this point, William Stanley led his men to the assistance of Henry, who climbed Crown Hill when he spotted the danger. Stanley's men surrounded Richard,

Bosworth sundial. (ARN Kinross)

Bosworth Field: King
Richard's Well.

Bosworth Field: inside there is
a memorial to King Richard
III. Northumberland's men left
their arms in a ditch near here
after Richard's death.

killed his horse and then him. Only Northumberland could now save the day, but he
saw what was happening, turned round and fled the field, his men throwing their arms
into a ditch close to Sutton Cheney Church.

William Stanley placed the fallen crown on Henry's head and the battle was over.
Almost 1,000 men had been killed. Richard's body was stripped, placed across a
horse and taken to Leicester. (Many years later it was discovered under a car park
and buried with a lot of ceremony in Leicester Cathedral.) Lord Strange was released
unharmed and Henry was crowned king. However, there were other rebellions and
William Stanley lost his life by supporting one of them. The most serious, by the Earl of
Lincoln, ended at the Battle of Stoke Field (see page 102).

## Bosworth Today

Take the A5 from London and turn right around half a mile (800 metres) before
Atherstone along an old Roman road to Sutton Cheney. In Sutton Cheney Church,
the Richard III Society has put up a monument to the former king with the following
inscription: 'Remember before God, Richard III, King of England, and those who fell
at Bosworth Field having kept faith 22 August 1485. Loyaulté Me Lie.'

The Battlefield Centre is an old well-signposted farm. Here is a shop, restaurant
in a barn, small museum and a new monument – basically a sundial with a crown
that indicates what happened hour by hour decorated with coloured roses. Dadlington
Church is close to Redesmere, where Richard was killed and in the small churchyard

many of the dead from both sides were buried. This is a place to take the whole family and be prepared to walk or cycle round the large battlefield. Cars are best left at the centre car park.

# 27. CLIFTON MOOR, 18 DECEMBER 1745

## Cumbria OS Landranger 90 (532 269)

After his victory at Prestonpans, Prince Charles Edward Stuart, the Young Pretender, marched his army south into England, taking Carlisle and continuing through Lancaster, Preston and Manchester to Derby. But support in England did not materialise. His Highlanders began to desert and, with large government armies approaching, the decision was made to retreat to Scotland.

The Jacobites retreated from Derby on 6 December. It was a disastrous step for their morale but, in the circumstances, a wise one. Field Marshal George Wade's government army was in a position to cut them off on the border and George II's younger son, the Duke of Cumberland, with 4,000 dragoons and around 3,000 infantry, blocked the road at Lichfield.

The retreat was a difficult business because of the state of the roads in winter and the slowness of the artillery and baggage. On 18 December Charles arrived at Penrith, but the artillery and rearguard were 6 miles (10 km) behind at Clifton, a small village on a slight hill. A collection of local militia, poorly armed but mounted, suddenly appeared on the road between Penrith and Clifton. Lord George Murray, commanding the

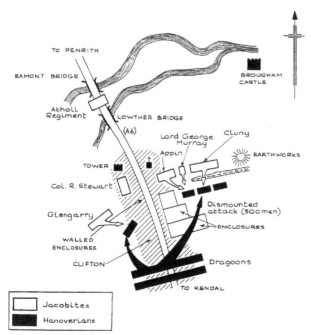

*Battle of Clifton Moor, 1745.*

Bland's regiment memorial in the churchyard. (ARN Kinross)

rearguard, which consisted of Macdonald of Glengarry's regiment, charged them and captured two men, one of whom was the Duke of Cumberland's servant. He informed Lord George that the duke and 4,000 men were hot on his heels, so a further three regiments – Cluny's MacPhersons, Colonel Roy Stewart's men and the Stewarts of Appin – were marched back to Clifton, where Lord George posted them behind the enclosed walls of the village. The artillery was sent on to Penrith and at 4 p.m. Cumberland's dragoons appeared – around 500 of them dismounted in two lines making for the enclosures. The duke had sent forward ten men from each platoon.

Lord George sent Cluny's men up to a thick hedge, which they burst through, and they fell upon the dragoons. The latter had time to fire once before the Jacobites led by Lord George, now hatless and wigless, were on them. Around twelve dragoons were killed and many wounded. The MacPhersons broke fourteen swords on the metal skullcaps of the Englishmen. 'We did very well,' said one Highlander after the fight, 'until the lang man in muckle boots came over the dyke.' This was Colonel Honeywood, commander of Bland's regiment (later the Queen's Own Hussars), who was badly wounded. His sword and those of the fallen were eagerly picked up by Cluny MacPherson's men.

Meanwhile the Glengarry Regiment had been positioned behind a stone wall overlooking the road, with the small regiment of Colonel Roy Stewart behind them as a rearguard. When a party of dragoons tried to take Cluny on the flank, they drove them off by their brisk fire. The white belts of the dragoons shone in the moonlight, but soon it was so dark that it became difficult to tell friend from foe.

Ultimately the dragoons retreated, leaving ten dead and many wounded, including the gallant Colonel Honeywood. Around four of Cluny's men were killed and around twelve captured because they pursued too far and ran into the main body of Cumberland's men drawn up on the moor. These prisoners were very unfortunate. Taken to York, a few were executed and others were sold as slaves to America. One of the latter returned to France and became a sergeant in the Regiment of Royal Scots. Honeywood recovered from his wounds and was later promoted to General of Horse.

Clifton Moor: Kelterwell, grille and battle memorial. (ARN Kinross)

The skirmish, for it was hardly a battle, was a triumph for Lord George Murray. The prince had given orders to retreat rather than risk action, but Lord George had disobeyed them to beat off the pursuit. The Duke of Perth, who had informed Charles personally of the presence of the dragoons, had sent the Atholl Regiment with some of his own men to Lowther Bridge under the Count of Nairn as a reinforcement but they were never used.

## Clifton Moor Today

The village of Clifton lies 6 miles (10 km) south of Penrith on the A6. In St Cuthbert's churchyard, to the right of the gate, is a headstone erected by the Queen's Own Hussars to the men of Bland's Regiment. The tower across the road from the church is Clifton Hall, a fifteenth-century structure in the care of English Heritage. It might have been used as a strongpoint during the fight. Opposite Cumberland Close, half a mile (800 metres) south of the church, is a commemorative seat and decorated metal grille. At Town End Farm there is an oak tree with a small monument to two Highlanders killed when they were cut off in the attack. The Bland's tombstone in the churchyard has been recently replaced by the Queen's Own Royal Hussars, who have a different badge to their predecessors.

# 28. EDGECOTE, 26 JULY 1469

Northamptonshire OS Landranger 151 (519 468)

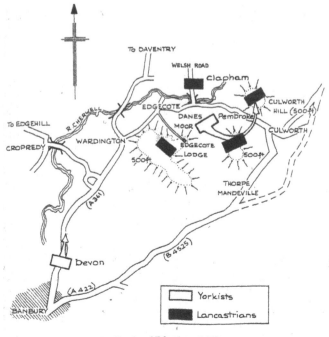

*Battle of Edgecote, 1469.*

The battles of Northampton and Towton put Edward IV on the throne, but he descended upon his allies the Earl of Warwick and the Nevilles to maintain the peace of England, and in those troubled years of the Wars of the Roses there was little peace for the nobility. In 1464 Edward married Elizabeth Woodville, the widow of a Lancastrian knight and daughter of the Duke of Bedford's steward. This rash step was followed by the rise of the Woodville family in court and government. When Edward married his sister to Charles of Burgundy, thus jeopardising England's relationship with France, it was too much for Warwick; he went to Calais with Edward's brother George, Duke of Clarence, and waited there, prepared to return and oppose Edward when the time was right.

In the north a new figure suddenly came onto the scene – Robin of Redesdale. Protesting against the 'thrave tax', Robin (who was actually a Yorkshire knight, Sir John Conyers) raised an army of bowmen under Warwick's banner of the ragged staff. When Clarence and Warwick landed at Sandwich in May, Robin had already moved south and Edward, with a very small army, went to Nottingham. Proclaiming that his daughter Isabel was to marry Clarence, Warwick now ordered Robin's troops to cut Edward off from London. Edward, realising his danger, summoned Sir William Herbert, Earl of Pembroke, and William's brother, Richard, from Wales, where they had recently captured Harlech Castle. A more formidable army of bowmen under Humphrey Stafford, newly created Earl of Devon, joined Pembroke and made for Northampton, where they had hoped to prevent Robin's army, then at Leicester, from linking up with Warwick's men, who had reached London in July.

On 25 July Devon and Pembroke quarrelled at Banbury about their billets, and Devon led his men away to Deddington, where they were protected in the castle, north of Banbury, near Wardington. On 26 July Pembroke, who was an experienced but somewhat foolhardy soldier, saw the Lancastrian army occupying three hills around his position. His way out of this would have been to withdraw to join Devon. Instead he attacked. With remarkable dash, his Welshmen captured the central hill and, turning left, attacked Culworth Hill. Young Richard Herbert twice passed through 'the battail of his adversaries without any mortal wound', killing many with his poleaxe. Robin's men received fresh supplies of arrows and those on Culworth Hill forced Pembroke back onto Danes Moor. Here he was out of bowshot range and his Welsh spearmen began to force back the advancing rebels. Warwick had meanwhile dispatched a small advance force under John Clapham of Skipton,

Edgecote House and
Church. (Author)

a veteran of Towton. Joined by some Northampton ruffians, Clapham suddenly appeared in Pembroke's rear with shouts of 'A Warwick, A Warwick', and the battle was over. Both Herberts were executed at Northampton. Lord Devon, who had arrived when it was all over, escaped to Somerset, where he was killed by an angry street mob. Robin's young son was killed, together with 168 knights, squires and gentlemen of both sides. Edward IV and his brother Richard had taken refuge at Olney. Here Warwick's brother, the Archbishop of York, captured them, and the Nevilles were supreme until defeated at Barnet in 1471.

## Edgecote Today

This is a beautiful part of Northamptonshire and the battlefield can be seen clearly by taking the A361 Daventry road out of Banbury to Wardington, turning right and driving round Danes Moor through Thorpe Mandeville and Culworth. Edgecote Lodge stands high on the hill overlooking Pembroke's position.

The road across the Cherwell and up to Aston le Walls is known as Welsh Road. It was the only escape route for the Welsh spearmen, and Hays Bridge, where Clapham appeared, is well concealed from Danes Moor.

# 29. EDGEHILL, 23 OCTOBER 1642

Warwickshire, OS Landranger 151 (357 492)

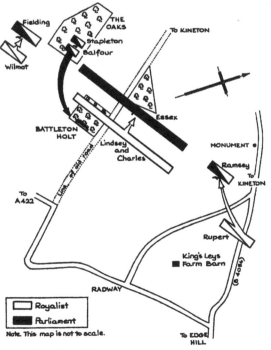

Battle of Edgehill, 1642.

King Charles I. (National Army Museum)

Stoke Field was the last major battle to be fought in England between two English armies until the Civil War, and in the intervening 155 years much change had taken place in warfare. Armour, apart from helmets and breastplates, was abandoned; infantry was armed with pikes and with muskets, some so heavy that they had to be fired on a crutch support; heavy cannon were introduced on the field, as were small sakers that fired grapeshot; and there were numerous other field guns. But more important than the artillery was the cavalry, armed with pistols and swords.

The accepted idea of cavalry tactics was the 'caracole'. This involved a brisk trot to around fifty yards (45 metres) from the enemy line, a barrage of pistols, then a swift retreat to make way for a barrage from the second line of horse. There was little contact or actual sword fighting. Prince Rupert introduced the Swedish methods of Gustavus Adolphus. Not all his men had pistols, and he told them to bunch together and gallop through the enemy position using pistols and swords only at close range.

When sides were taken in the Civil War, King Charles I found support among a majority of the House of Lords and just over a third of the Commons, the majority of the country gentry, the Catholics and the universities. The Puritans, the expanding trading classes, the City of London and the Royal Navy supported Parliament. The closing of the ports to foreign aid weighted the scales heavily against the king from the outset. Geographically, the poorer parts of the country, the northern counties, Wales and the West Country, supported the king, while the eastern counties south of the Humber, southern England, the cloth districts of the West Riding and Somerset and all the main seaports supported Parliament.

Both sides secured generals who had some experience of war. The king was served by his brilliant nephew Prince Rupert of the Palatinate in Germany (who could probably have won the war if he had been allowed to), Sir Ralph Hopton, Lord Goring and the Earl (later Marquis) of Newcastle. Parliamentary leaders were Robert Devereux, Earl of Essex, Sir William Waller and the Earl of Manchester and, later, Sir Thomas Fairfax and Oliver Cromwell.

Both armies were initially badly organised. There was a reluctance of local levies to leave their counties unprotected, and on the Royalist side there was too much concentration on the maintenance of small scattered garrisons. At first the king had the great advantage of superb cavalry contributed by the nobility, while Parliament had the only reasonably competent infantry in the country, the London trained bands.

Edgehill battlefield. Castle Inn is on the skyline. (ARN Kinross)

Charles I, having raised his standard at Nottingham in August 1642, proceeded to Shrewsbury collecting troops. The Parliamentary army under the Earl of Essex moved out of London towards Nottingham; Charles moved to Chester, and Prince Rupert went on to Worcester, where he defeated a force of Roundhead cavalry at Powick Bridge. The Earl of Essex reached Worcester and Charles, inspired by Rupert's success, blocked his retreat at Edgehill. The hill rises 600 feet (182 metres) for 3 miles (5 km) in a boomerang shape, the long arm looking over towards the Kineton plain, the rear overlooking the Warwick–Stratford road and Essex's route to London. It was, and still is, a commanding spot.

Charles had over 13,000 men, Essex slightly fewer. Rupert was on the right wing facing Ramsey's horse, and Wilmot faced Fielding's horse on the left. Essex, however, had placed a cavalry reserve under Balfour, a capable Scottish soldier, and Stapleton, in a wood behind his infantry. The Royalists had descended from the hill before the battle and, when Rupert charged, the impetus of his horse and his superiority in numbers meant that he carried all before him. Wilmot met with similar success on the other flank, and a chase to Kineton and beyond developed.

The infantry in the centre fought behind hedges, neither side gaining ground until Balfour's cavalry charged the centre regiment, cutting through them and sweeping into Battleton Holt, a small copse where the Royalist heavy guns were positioned. There was no means of capturing the guns, so Balfour contented himself with cutting their traces and killing the gunners. The Roundhead line now wheeled to the right, and a great hand-to-hand fight took place round the royal standard, which was captured; Sir Edmund Verney, the standard-bearer, was killed and Charles's general, the Earl of Lindsey, mortally wounded. The king was now in difficulties and only the weariness of the enemy and the reappearance of some of the cavalry prevented his retreat. One of the returning horsemen, Captain John Smith, saw a group of Balfour's men making off with the standard. He charged them alone, killing one with his sword and wounding another. The rest fled and the royal standard was returned to the king. Captain Smith was knighted the following morning.

Charles spent the night in the barn of King's Leys Farm, his troops remaining in their positions. Essex collected his men with difficulty and withdrew next day to Warwick, leaving the road to London open for Charles, who entered Oxford, his headquarters for the remainder of the war, in triumph.

Edgehill: a re-enactment of the battle by the Sealed Knot. (The Sealed Knot)

The first campaign of the war now took the form of a race between the armies of Charles and Essex for London, but Charles delayed his march on London too long and, although Rupert's advance guard captured Brentford, the combined forces of Essex, who had not delayed, and the trained bands of London waiting at Turnham Green forced the king to withdraw to winter quarters in Oxford.

## Edgehill Today

Leave Banbury by the B4100 to Warwick. Turn left after 7 miles (11 km) on the B4086. Continue down the hill towards Kineton (pronounced 'Kine-ton'). There is a small monument on the left of the road half a mile (800 metres) after a level crossing. The battlefield itself is Ministry of Defence property. In Radway Church is a mutilated monument to Captain Kingswell, a Royalist killed in the battle. The steep hill is impressive, although in 1642 there were no trees on the ridge. The view from the top of Castle Inn on Edge Hill gives one the best impression of Charles' view on the morning of the battle.

# 30. EVESHAM, 4 AUGUST 1265

Worcestershire OS Landranger 150 (035 452)

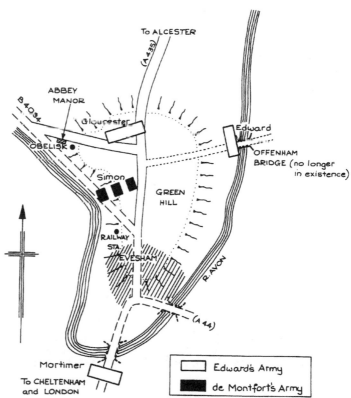

Battle of Evesham, 1265.

After Lewes, Simon de Montfort looked for allies in Wales and found one in a local patriot, Llewellyn, whose Welsh territory he recognised. By doing this he made many enemies, one of whom, Gilbert de Clare, Earl of Gloucester, raised a force of horsemen in the Welsh Marches. This small army suddenly became important when Prince Edward, still a prisoner of de Montfort, escaped in a hunting party and joined Gloucester in May, 1265.

One of Simon's sons, also called Simon, was in Kenilworth with a small force and, when later in the summer Edward's army appeared at Worcester, de Montfort set out from Hereford in order to join his son at Kenilworth. On 3 August he reached Evesham, camping at a bend in the river. Early the following morning a barber on the church tower spotted the banners of the younger Simon advancing from Alcester. Another force was crossing Offenham Bridge. Another under Mortimer blocked the bridge on the London road. It took Simon a few minutes to realise that he was surrounded and that disaster had overtaken his son. By a brilliant long march two days earlier Edward had surprised young Simon at Kenilworth. He then turned around to march on Evesham and divided his army into three groups to block de Montfort's escape routes, using captured banners to deceive him.

Simon's army was around 5,000 and Edward's and Gloucester's forces amounted to twice the size. 'May God have mercy on our souls,' said de Montfort when he learnt this, 'for our bodies are theirs.' With a bold decision he arranged his army in a tight group, the few horsemen in front, the English foot next and the Welsh foot in the rear. There was a heavy downpour and it was a dark morning; with luck Simon might slip between Edward and Gloucester and escape towards Alcester.

Perched on Green Hill, Edward could see the enemy's position in spite of the weather. His line recoiled under Simon's charge, but the extended wings surrounded

*Above left*: Evesham: the tomb of Simon de Montfort in All Saints Churchyard. (ARN Kinross)

*Above right*: Evesham: the death of Simon de Montfort. (Grant)

the smaller army. Many of the Welsh swam the river and escaped but Simon and most of the English foot were killed where they stood.

Kenilworth Castle held out for many months for the de Montfort cause. King Henry III, who had been Simon's captive and was nearly killed by Prince Edward's men at Evesham, pursued a policy of moderation. When Edward came to the throne, he carried on Simon's political ideas. Parliament grew in strength, the common law was respected and justice prevailed.

## Evesham Today

Coming into Evesham on the A44, take the right-hand turn by Chadbury Farm Shop. Opposite is a stile leading to the Leicester Tower and a path takes you to the monument. The Abbey Manor is now divided into ten flats, so the main entrance is for residents only.

The obelisk is in the garden, hidden behind a lily pond. This overlooks the site of the battle and is inscribed, 'On this spot in the reign of Henry III the Battle of Evesham was fought August IV, 1262, between the king's forces commanded by his eldest son Prince Edward and the Barons under Simon de Montfort, Earl of Leicester, in which the Prince, by his skill and valour, obtained a complete victory.' There is a picture of the king's narrow escape from death on the other side. Many of the Welsh were killed at Dead Men's Ait, a meadow opposite the Bridge Inn at Offenham. The stone bridge was demolished in Victorian times. The de Montfort room in the local museum should not be missed. There is a recent tomb to Simon in the churchyard next to the museum.

# 31. FLODDEN, 9 SEPTEMBER 1513

## Northumberland OS Landranger 74 (890 370)

'No Scottish army had even taken the field so well equipped,' wrote a Scottish historian about the 40,000 men with whom King James IV crossed into England in 1513. Henry VIII had taken a large army to France, and the French king, Louis XII, had called on his traditional Scottish allies for help. The young Henry had left a small army in England in the hands of the Earl of Surrey who, although over seventy and a veteran of Richard III's defeated army at Bosworth, was an experienced leader who knew the border country well. Setting out for the Tweed Valley, where the Scots had captured Ford Castle, Surrey collected his army en route. It amounted to around 26,000 men but included a large force of archers. His men-at-arms had short bills and halberds while the Scots had 15-foot (4.6-metre) French pikes.

At Alnwick a party of armed 'sailors' under Lord Thomas Howard, Surrey's oldest son, joined the English army and precise instructions were given to the men on the tactics to be employed. Howard was appointed second-in-command. The Scottish army was strongly positioned on Flodden Edge near the river Till. Surrey sent Roger Croix, his herald, to King James to suggest the time and place of

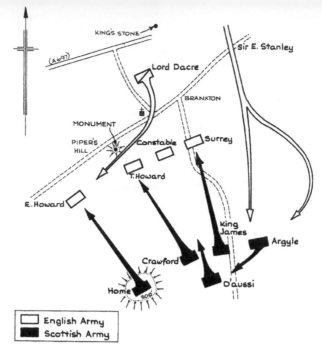

*Battle of Flodden, 1513.*

the forthcoming battle, but the Scots king was not prepared for this old-fashioned method and replied that he would fight when and where he chose. Undaunted, Surrey divided his army and on 9 September, in the pouring rain, moved east and circled round the Scots position, crossing the Till at Twizel and Milford bridges so as to cut off the Scottish retreat.

It was a bold move, and James could have caught him on the flank when his army was divided. Instead he turned his men round and took up a defensive position on Branxton Hill facing north. His artillery, under Borthwick, was the most modern in Europe but he could not advance quickly without leaving it behind. The smoke from his camp fires at Flodden prevented the English from observing his movements. The English vanguard under Lord Thomas Howard had to cross Pallin's Burn in a column with bogland on either side. No sooner had they been deployed than James's borderers under Lord Home charged. The English right wing under Edmund Howard was swept aside and Howard was wounded. The English artillery, which had crossed the bog at Sandyford, now came into its own. The Scottish king formed his men into schiltrons, massed circles of pikemen around their standards, and the two centre divisions, led by Crawford and James himself, advanced on Surrey and his son. On the English side, Lord Dacre, who had been stationed behind with his horsemen in reserve, attacked the borderers in the flank and drove them off. Their leader, Lord Home, was later executed for treachery in failing to bring in his reserves against the English horsemen, but his ruffians were so busy plundering the dead that he was unable to rally them.

The English rearguard under Sir Edward Stanley then appeared on the flank of the unengaged Scottish division. While holding their attention with part of his force, Stanley sent his archers round out of sight to fire at their flank. These Scots, mostly poorly armed Highlanders, turned and fled. Stanley now attacked the main Scottish force in the rear while Dacre charged from the right flank. James, reinforced by his French reserve under the Comte d'Aussi, fought bravely, but at last a halberd thrust killed him. It was a victory for the English halberd over the unwieldy pike and heavy

Flodden: King James's view from
Flodden Hill. (ARN Kinross)

sword. Five thousand Scots, including their king and three bishops, were slaughtered. The Earl of Surrey, who had been mocked by the Scots as 'the old crooked earl in a chariot' because his gout forced him to travel by coach, regained his Norfolk dukedom, and henceforward Henry VIII had no more trouble with Scotland.

## Flodden Today

A simple stone monument to the dead of both nations marks the site of the battle. To get to it, take the A697 from Morpeth north to Coldstream and turn off before the Tweed Bridge to the village of Branxton. The monument is on a small hill above the church and the view around is outstanding. There is a small car park and in 2013 a trail was made going round the field with the monument and containing several interpretation boards. This is easy to follow for walkers. However, there were so many soldiers taking part that it should not be forgotten that the actual battle took many times the space of the field, but it is a start. There is also an interpretation map inside Branxton telephone box.

# 32. HEDGELEY MOOR, 25 APRIL 1464

## Northumberland OS Landranger 81 (049 197)

The rout of the Lancastrians at Towton was not the end of the Lancastrian army. It retreated north and occupied Skipton and Norham castles. Sir Ralph Percy attempted to put himself in charge of a Lancastrian force that camped near Wooler in April 1464. He had little success in raising new recruits, but with the help of Lord Roos and Lord Hungerford he raised around 1,500 men. Meanwhile the Yorkists had left a force in Newcastle upon Tyne under Warwick's younger brother, Lord Montagu. It is likely that Montagu had spies in the Lancastrian camp because he caught up with them at Hedgeley Moor, near Wooler, on 25 April.

Sir Ralph Percy was undaunted by the oncoming Yorkist army, but Roos and Hungerford and their supporters retreated to Hexham. Percy, who had positioned himself on the right wing, spurred his horse straight at Montagu, knowing that if he

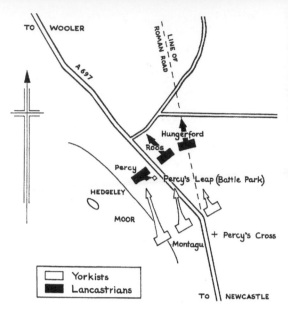

*Battle of Hedgeley Moor, 1464.* The Percy Cross. (Author)

killed their leader the Yorkists would be defeated. According to tradition, the horse made a terrific leap – the spot is known today as Percy's Leap – and both horse and rider were wounded. The latter's wound was mortal but before he died Percy was heard to say, 'I have saved the bird in my bosom.' It was a confession that he had died for the rightful monarch, after temporarily deserting him. Montagu's men soon mopped up the rest of the Lancastrian army, though at Hexham Roos and Hungerford joined forces with the Duke of Somerset (son of the duke killed at the first battle of St Albans). Here they were finally defeated by Montagu in May. Queen Margaret, however, survived to fight again.

## Hedgeley Moor Today

Northumberland County Council has made a small battle enclosure by the A697 with two boulders representing the leap by Percy's horse. More interesting is the Percy Cross in a railed enclosure around 500 yards (450 metres) further south on the other side of the road. It stands on private land and on it are the arms of Percy and Lucy. It is a much grander affair than that at Otterburn and appears to have been in two pieces at one time.

# 33. HOMILDON HILL, 14 SEPTEMBER 1402

## Northumberland OS Landranger 75 (969 295)

In the summer of 1402 King Henry IV took an army to Wales and during his absence a Scottish army of nearly 10,000 men under Archibald, Earl of Douglas, and Murdoch Stewart, son of the Duke of Albany, crossed the border, laying waste to Northumberland as far as the Tyne.

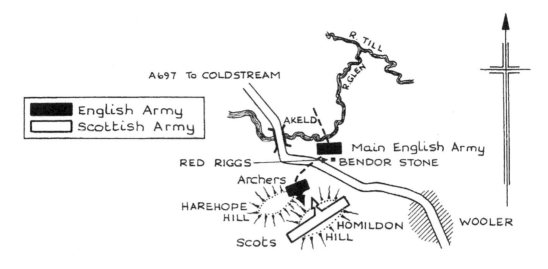

*Battle of Homildon Hill, 1402.*

The English commander in the north was Sir Henry Percy, Earl of Northumberland, and he raised an army with his son Hotspur and the refugee Earl of March, a Scot out of league with Douglas and Albany. Percy's army set out from Dunstanburgh to Wooler, where they camped north of the village on the River Till in a position that would block the passage of the Scots when they returned towards Coldstream and the border.

Douglas reached Wooler before his scouts gave him warning of the English army, so he drew up his ranks on the flat-topped Homildon Hill just outside Wooler. Percy had detached his 500 archers and positioned them on the opposite hill. By firing in ranks and withdrawing, the archers carefully lured the Scots down to a field known as Red Riggs, where the mounted English horsemen were ready for them. The Scots, angered by the English archers, probably outnumbered the English but their archers had short bows that did not have the range to reach the English ranks. Sir John Swinton, a border knight, and Sir Adam Gordon, who for many years had been his rival, led a Scottish charge of 100 lances but it was cut down by the heavily armed English troops. Douglas himself was wounded and captured along with Murdoch Stewart and the earls of Moray, Angus and Orkney.

The Red Riggs valley between Homildon and Harehope Hills and the Bendor Stone. (Author)

The retreated Scots were pursued as far as Coldstream, where many were killed crossing the Tweed. The English longbow was the real winner of Homildon but the Scottish prisoners led to the downfall of Hotspur. He refused to give them up to the king, and the wily Douglas persuaded him to attempt to join forces with Owen Glyndwyr's Welsh army. The following year thus saw the eclipse of both Hotspur and Douglas at Shrewsbury, the battle at which the young Prince Henry won his spurs.

## Homildon Hill Today

The hill marked on the map as Humbleton Hill is 2 miles (3 km) north-west of Wooler. Red Riggs fields is on the other side of the A697 and a battle stone, called the Bendor Stone, stands in it. The English archers were probably on Harehope Hill and descended to the river near Akeld, where they joined the main English force that had crossed the river. There is another battle stone between Yeavering and Old Yeavering, but as bones have been dug up at Red Riggs it is assumed that this is where the main action took place.

# 34. MARSTON MOOR, 2 JULY 1644

## North Yorkshire OS Landranger 105 (491 525)

Despite the Royalist success at Newark, the Scottish Army, in alliance with Parliament and under the Earl of Leven, was still besieging the Marquis of Newcastle in York.

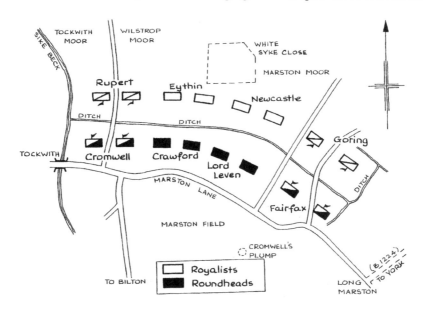

*Battle of Marston Moor, 1644.*

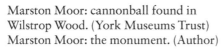

Marston Moor: cannonball found in
Wilstrop Wood. (York Museums Trust)
Marston Moor: the monument. (Author)

Sir Thomas Fairfax and the Earl of Manchester commanded the Parliamentary troops, and their total allied force amounted to 27,000 men. Prince Rupert, with 12,000 troops, arrived at Preston. On 23 June he left for Skipton, and the alarmed allied commanders decided to break off the siege and concentrate their forces west of York on the barren moor between the villages of Tockwith and Long Marston. On 30 June the Royalists reached Knaresborough and Rupert devised a bold plan: he sent a small cavalry squadron to make a disturbance at Tockwith and with the rest of his army he left early on 1 July for Boroughbridge. Crossing the River Ure, he made for Thornton Bridge over the Swale near Brafferton and, turning south-east, headed for York, protected from the enemy by the Ouse. At Nether Poppleton he surprised some dragoons guarding a pontoon bridge and, crossing his third river, arrived on the outskirts of York. The Marquis sent a letter of congratulation via Lord Goring, who had gone on ahead. Elated by his initial success, Rupert ordered an attack the following day.

'The Prince has done his work,' wrote Clarendon, 'and if he had sat still the other great army would have mouldered.' The Scots and English on the moor were running short of water. The men squabbled with each other, and discipline in the Scottish Army was poor. Lord Leven ordered the foot to march south to hold the bridge at Tadcaster, and when Rupert arrived at Long Marston he was without his infantry because they were plundering the abandoned siege lines. Lord Eythin, who was second in command of the Whitecoats, as Newcastle's troops were known because of their undyed serge jackets (they vowed to dye them in the blood of the enemy), had been with Rupert at Lemgo in Germany, where he had failed to prevent the Prince from being taken prisoner. Now his late arrival had prevented an attack that would have caught the allies at a disadvantage.

By four in the afternoon the positions were ready. Rupert's own cavalry faced Cromwell's horse for the first time. Lord Goring faced Sir Thomas Fairfax on the Marston wing and the foot, as at Edgehill, were in the centre. Between the two armies was a ditch lined by Royalist musketeers. On the allied left wing the ditch was partially filled in, so Cromwell's cavalry had an advantageous position. At half past seven

Marston Moor:
Cromwell's Plump.
(Author)

the weather changed and when the Royalist commanders were eating their supper, simultaneously with a clap of thunder, the whole allied line advanced.

Marston Moor was a very confused battle. Manchester's chaplain, Simon Ash, standing at the group of trees still known as Cromwell's Plump, saw only 'so many thick clouds'. Lord Byron, commanding the front line of Rupert's cavalry, was forced back, but one of his officers, Colonel Trevor, hit out with his sword and caught Cromwell at the back of his neck, forcing the Parliamentary leader to retire to have his wound dressed. David Leslie, in charge of the second line of Parliamentary cavalry, attacked Rupert's horse in the flank and after a brief fight the Royalists were driven off the field. On the other wing, Fairfax had been sharply dealt with by both musketeers and by gorse bushes. His troops were soon forced back by Goring but he himself, wounded in the face, went on to attempt to circle the rear of the Royalist position and join up with Cromwell. In spite of losing his horse, he succeeded in this manoeuvre, pretending to be a Royalist by removing his white hat band.

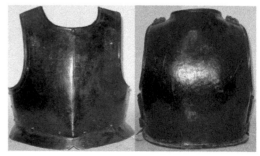

*Left*: Marston Moor: Thomas Fairfax. (Grant)

*Above*: Armour worn by a trooper of Prince Rupert's cavalry found on the battlefield. (York Museum Trust)

Cromwell returned to the fray and, stirred on by the angry words of Lawrence Crawford, who commanded Manchester's foot, he joined Fairfax and attacked Goring, who had to turn about to meet his enemy. The whole line had now moved round clockwise so that Newcastle was nearly surrounded. 'The runaways were so many ... both armies being mingled, horses and foot, no side keeping their own posts,' wrote an observer. Scots were fleeing on one side and Royalists on the other. Cromwell's third and final charge won the day and the Whitecoats, whose leader had left them to their fate in White Syke Close, fought to the bitter end. The total killed was 4,000 Royalists and around 1,000 allies. Prince Rupert, who had been forced to hide in a bean field to escape the final rout, took the Royalist stragglers to Chester. York surrendered on 16 July and the Marquis of Newcastle fled to Holland and took no further part in the Civil War.

## Marston Moor Today

Take the B1224 from York towards Wetherby and in Long Marston turn right to Tockwith. An obelisk commemorating the battle is a little further along the Tockwith road. On the left after Long Marston is Cromwell's Plump, which can be reached by a footpath. There is a fine view of the battlefield from here. A model of the battle and Civil War arms can be seen in York Castle museum.

# 35. MORTIMER'S CROSS, 2 FEBRUARY 1461

Herefordshire OS Landranger 149 (427 637)

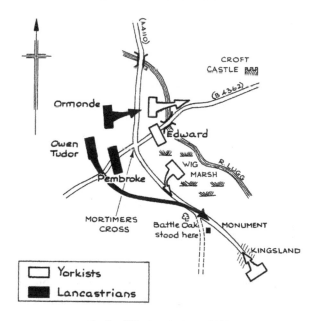

*Battle of Mortimer's Cross, 1461.*

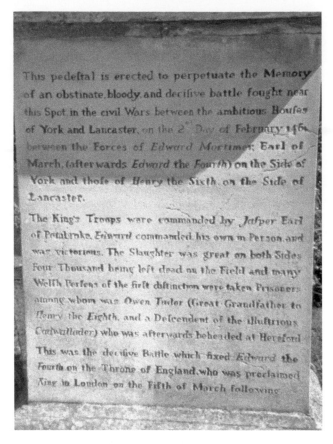

Mortimer's Cross: the monument to the battle. (Author)

The loss of his father and elder brother at Wakefield on 31 December 1460 must have been a terrible shock for the eighteen-year-old Edward, Earl of March. He heard the dreadful news at Shrewsbury, where he had spent Christmas, and then travelled to Gloucester. Jasper Tudor, Earl of Pembroke, and the Earl of Ormonde (also known as the Earl of Wiltshire), with their army of French, Irish and Welsh soldiers, many of whom had crossed to Wales from France, were determined to capture him. The Earl of Warwick was in London preparing to lead the Yorkists north against Queen Margaret, so Edward had to rely on his faithful 'Marchers', mostly farmers from the Welsh border, many of whom were well mounted but poorly armed.

The Lancastrians were marching east towards Worcester to try to get between Edward and Warwick. Moving north through Hereford, Edward, who must have been well served by scouts, placed his small army in Wig Marsh, north of Leominster, overlooking the Lugg River and the road junction now known as Mortimer's Cross. In the early morning of 2 February, his men were startled by the strange sight of three suns in the sky. Taking this as a religious omen representing the Trinity, the Yorkists knelt in prayer. They rose to find that the three suns were now one and that the vanguard of the Lancastrians was approaching.

The battle started at daybreak and continued until dusk. Edward held his ground. Sir Richard Croft, who lived at nearby Croft Castle, knew the lie of the land well and advised Edward to let the enemy attack. Pembroke put Ormonde's vanguard against Edward's right wing and sent the main body of his troops against Edward's centre. Ormonde's men chased Edward's off the field but by the time they returned to help Pembroke, the latter had been defeated. Three thousand men lay dead. The grandfather of Henry VII, Owen Tudor, was captured by the local Leominster men in the village of Kingsland. His son, Pembroke, escaped with the Earl of Ormonde towards Hereford. Owen Tudor was executed in Hereford marketplace. 'That head shall lie on the stock that was wont to lie on Queen Katherine's lap,' he said as he mounted the scaffold. He was the second husband of the mother of Henry VI, so he was a notable Lancastrian loss.

Just over two weeks later the Earl of Warwick was beaten at St Albans by the queen and the king was rescued. Edward, hurrying east to help, met the luckless Warwick and his survivors at Chipping Norton in Oxfordshire. Owen Tudor's death had delayed Edward sufficiently from riding to help Warwick. Margaret was in command, but the stage was set for the largest battle of the Wars of the Roses, at Towton.

## Mortimer's Cross Today

The monument erected in 1799 is at the junction of the A4110 from Hereford and the B4360 from Leominster, by the rugby club. There is no sign today of the Battle Oak that stood nearby. The crossroads is 1.5 miles (2 KM) to the north. Edward would have occupied the west bank of the Lugg and his scouts at Mortimer's Rock, south-west on the Shobdon Road, could have signalled to him on Pembroke's approach. Nearby Croft Castle is open to the public, and Sir Richard Croft's memorial is in the church. He died in 1507 and was a veteran of the battles of Tewkesbury and Stoke as well as Mortimer's Cross.

Inside Kingsland Church is the Volka Chapel, with an empty tomb that might have been prepared for one of the dead of the battle. Pevsner suggests that it was for Roger Mortimer's daughter, who married Thomas de Berkely in 1320 and was buried in what is now Bristol Cathedral in 1337. I noticed a kneeler there decorated by a parhelion – three suns – seen by Edward on the morning of the battle, which he took as a good omen and added to his badge of the White Rose.

Volka Chapel,
Mortimer's Cross and
a kneeler with the
three suns. (Author)

# 36. MYTON, 20 SEPTEMBER 1319

North Yorkshire OS Landranger 99 (432 688)

In 1318 the Scots moved south and captured Berwick-upon-Tweed. The English army, or what was left of it, moved up to besiege it, but King Edward II and his young queen, Isabella, remained in York. The Scots had a plan to capture her and held her to ransom. Like so many Scottish armies that moved south, they soon ran out of money and looked for all sorts of methods to feed their troops.

The River Swale flows through Swaledale to Richmond, then down towards York, east of the Great North Road, joining the River Ure just south of the village of Myton-on-Swale, where it is crossed by a small bridge 13 miles (21 km) north of York. This was a farming area even in the fourteenth century, and there were haystacks around as the fields had been harvested.

The Scots under Douglas bypassed Berwick and moved south. At Myton they camped in a field. One of their number was captured and taken to the Mayor of York who, with William de Melton, Archbishop of York, had raised a scratch English army from volunteers, mostly armed with sticks and hunting bows. This force, some 5,000 at the most, made for Myton, where there was a pall of smoke because the Scots had set fire to the haystacks to conceal their army from the oncoming English. It must have been a fearful sight for the untrained men to find their enemy in battle array with knights and spearmen in the centre and the hobilars, or mounted infantry, on the wings. The mayor and archbishop could not control their volunteers and the English took to their heels. According to records, around 4,000 were killed trying to cross the bridge to safety, many falling into the Swale.

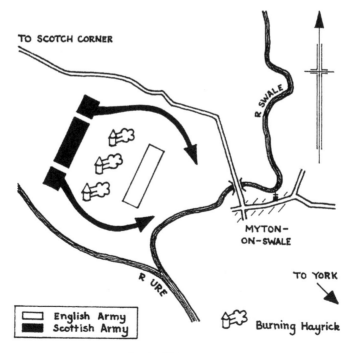

*Battle of Myton, 1319.*

The Scots did not occupy York, although there was nothing to stop them. Edward II was forced to sign a truce, the siege of Berwick was abandoned and for two years there was an uneasy peace.

## Myton Today

To reach Myton from York, take the A19, 10 miles (16 km) north to Easingwold, then turn left to Brafferton and Helperby, where the road goes south to Myton, which is a dead end. In 1319 a bridge here carried a main road north. A new brick and metal bridge has been built with two metal signs – one with bridge details and the other explaining the battle. There is a neat footpath round the battlefield, now ploughed up when we called in March 2016 – for the first time since the war when it was ploughed by horses. There is no car park here but cyclists and walkers are encouraged.

# 37. NANTWICH, 25 JANUARY 1644

## Cheshire OS Landranger 118 (635 535)

Parliamentary General Monck, a Royalist captured at Nantwich. He was the power behind the Restoration of 1660. (Granta)

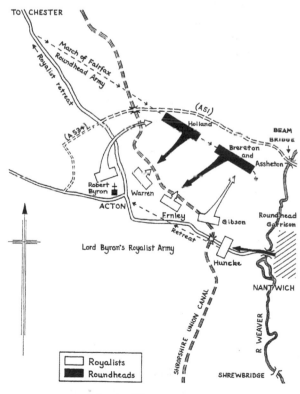

*Battle of Nantwich, 1644.*

In 1643 the Royalists under Lord Byron controlled most of Cheshire, an important county for them because Irish recruits landed at Hoylake, which was a useful port even forty-five years later when William of Orange used it to ferry his army to Ireland before the Boyne campaign. Holyhead in Anglesey was also a vital port for the king. Byron's army at Chester in late November 1643 consisted of 1,000 horse, mostly from Oxford, and 4,000 foot, mostly Irish. In Nantwich the Parliamentarians had a small garrison but its defender, Sir George Booth, now had 2,000 men and had used the River Weaver as a blockade, breaking the bridge at Beambridge, so that Byron, after capturing Beeston Castle, had to divide his army into two groups. The foot and artillery remained on the west bank, or Chester side, but the horse and some foot crossed by a temporary bridge to the east bank. The weather was terrible and during the night of 24 January this plank bridge was washed away, leaving Byron without his cavalry.

Meanwhile Sir Thomas Fairfax, with help from Sir William Brereton and Colonel Ralph Assheton, had gathered a relieving force of around 2,500 foot, 500 dragoons and 1,800 horse in Manchester. He set off to relieve Nantwich, reaching Tilston Heath, 8 miles (13 km) away, on 24 January. A small horse squadron sent out by Byron was captured at Delamere, but presumably one or two got back to him to inform him that the enemy was nigh. Byron drew up his foot at Acton Church. Leaving them under the command of Sir Michael Ernley, Colonel Henry Warren and Major General Gibson, he took command of the horse, some of which had now arrived from the east bank. He sent his musketeers under Sir Fulke Hunke to stop the garrison getting out of Nantwich while he watched with some surprise as Fairfax's men attempted to pass along the Tarporley–Nantwich road (now the A51) to get into the town. It was a rash move, and had Byron been a Prince Rupert or a Cromwell he would have routed Fairfax. However, part of the Irish foot deserted to Fairfax and the Royalist centre nearly broke but rallied round Lieutenant (later General) Monck. Hunke's men were driven to all parts by a successful Parliamentary sortie from Nantwich. Byron and his brother Robert, with most of the cavalry, escaped to Chester, but 1,500 foot surrendered at Acton Church, most of them preferring to join the Parliamentary army rather than become prisoners.

Nantwich was a decisive victory for Parliament and virtually brought the Irish recruiting to an end for the king. The Royalist cause in Cheshire was briefly revived when Prince Rupert came to the area before Marston Moor, but henceforward the county was controlled by Parliament. The battle of Rowton Heath in September 1645 forced the surrender of Byron in February 1646.

## Nantwich Today

The best approach to the battlefield is along the A51. At Hurleston, Fairfax spotted the Royalists at Acton Church. Turn left at the junction with the A534 and cross the Shropshire Union Canal. The canal crosses the battlefield and leads to Acton footbridge and Acton Church. There is a tomb here to Sir Richard Wilbraham, 1643, who lived at nearby Dorford Hall and may have died during the siege. The town of Nantwich has a Monk Street and a museum. Nantwich is not one of the battlefields on the English Heritage Battlefield Register, but it still has some green fields and is worthy of inclusion.

# 38. NASEBY, 14 JUNE 1645

Northampton OS Landranger 141 (682 801)

At the beginning of 1645, Parliament had gained decisive victories in the north at Marston Moor and in the south at Cheriton. Victory against King Charles himself had eluded them and the Royalists still held the south-west. After a period of drastic reorganisation in the high command, removing all who, like the Earl of Manchester, were reluctant to beat the king in battle, the New Model Army under Sir Thomas Fairfax was formed at Windsor.

In May Prince Rupert, who was now the Royalist commander-in-chief, attacked and captured Leicester while Fairfax and the New Model Army besieged Oxford. Moving south, some of King Charles' vanguard were captured at an inn in the village of Naseby. Charles called a council during the night and early next morning Rupert, who had wanted to join forces with Lord Goring's cavalry in the west before fighting, moved forward towards Naseby, finding on Dust Hill an ideal position to line up his troops with the wind behind them to blow smoke into the enemy. It was time to avenge Marston Moor.

The New Model Army, greatly superior in numbers, had also found a ridge on which to form their line of battle. Oliver Cromwell's three lines of cavalry were on the right facing Sir Marmaduke Langdale's Northern Horse; Philip Skippon, the veteran of Newbury, 1643, was in the centre with the infantry and opposite Lord Astley and Charles, while on the right stood Henry Ireton's horse facing Rupert and Prince Maurice. The start of the battle was like Edgehill all over again. Rupert's fierce charge drove most of Ireton's horse off the field and only the musketeers round the baggage train behind forced the Cavaliers back. Astley's infantry advanced on Skippon, who was wounded,

*Above*: Philip Skippon. (National Army Museum)
*Right*: Battle of Naseby, 1645.

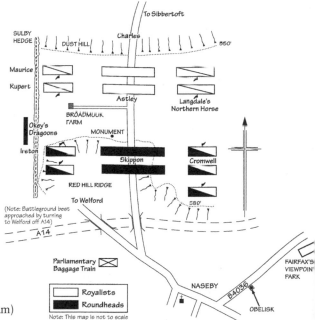

Naseby: Cromwell's monument. (Author)

but they in turn were charged by Ireton himself with a troop of horse that had not fled from Rupert, and also by John Okey's dragoons. Ireton was captured and, if it had not been for Cromwell, Charles might have carried off an overwhelming victory.

Cromwell's first troop under Edward Whalley advanced on Langdale, whose inferior horsemen were driven off the field. Cromwell himself charged with his own troop in a left wheel on the flank of Astley's infantry. Charles, trying to intervene with his reserve, was forestalled by the Earl of Carnwath, who seized his rein and shouted, 'Will you go upon your death?' Rupert, returning, realised the situation was hopeless and fled with the king to Leicester and Ashby de la Zouch Castle.

Astley's men laid down their arms. Only Rupert's Bluecoats fought to the bitter end. By lunchtime the battle was over. Fairfax had captured the royal baggage, which included all of Charles' correspondence and around £100,000 in gold, silver and jewels. Some 4,000 cavalry remained to the king, but all Astley's foot had been killed, wounded or captured. On 17 June Leicester surrendered to Fairfax. Cromwell, who on

'grounds of moral principle' closed his eyes to the slaughter of some 200 women camp-followers, could well declare that Naseby was a victory 'of which I had great assurance and God did it'.

The king's cause was lost and he finally gave himself up to the Scots in May 1646, a year in which only Montrose, in Scotland and the north, was to see success for the Royalists.

The battle obelisk. (Author)

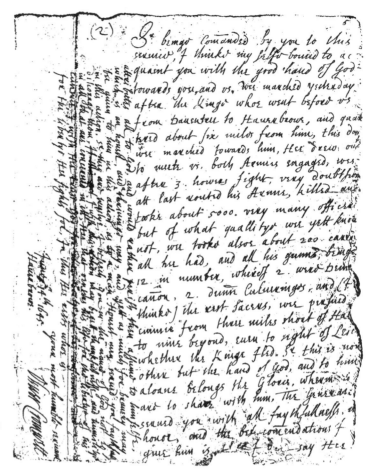

Cromwell's letter to Parliament
with the news of Naseby.
(State Papers)

## Naseby Today

Between Northampton and Market Harborough off the A50, Naseby village is
600 feet (180 metres) above sea level and close to the source of the Avon. Take the
Welford road north-west from Naseby, turning right to Sibbertoft almost immediately.
The first ridge marks the Roundhead position, where there is a monument. It was
put up in 1936, supposedly, but incorrectly, showing the starting point of Cromwell's
charge. Broadmoor Farm below is near where Rupert charged. The Royalist slope is
not so steep. An obelisk on the B4036 near Naseby village, put up in 1923 by the lord
of the manor, states that the battle 'led to the subversion of the throne, the altar and the
constitution … leaving a useful lesson to British kings never to exceed the bounds of
their prerogative'.

The A14 is now bridged so the best approach to the battlefield is via Welford. There
is a small car park at Fairfax's view between Welford and Naseby, then the obelisk
(placed in 1823 where there was once a windmill). Finally, the Cromwell monument
is at the corner of the battlefield where Cromwell is supposed to have started his
charge. The map by the obelisk shows a battle trail and on Sundays in summer the Old
Vicarage, Naseby, does teas.

# 39. NEVILLE'S CROSS, 17 OCTOBER 1346

## County Durham OS Landranger 88 (261 420)

In August 1346, Edward III led his army in France to a great victory over Philip VI of France at Crécy. The French king, in despair, called upon his ally David II of Scotland to invade England and give him a respite. The English army in the north was commanded by the Archbishop of York, Lord Neville of Raby and Henry, Lord Percy. An army of at least 15,000 men was assembled at a summons to arms at Bishop Auckland and moved north to attack the Scots, somewhat superior in numbers, who were camped at Beaurepair Abbey outside Durham.

Surprising the Scottish vanguard at Sunderland Bridge, Neville, who was in command, led his army on to Red Hill. On the left were the Archbishop and Sir Thomas Rokeby and on the right Lord Percy. Each division had a small troop of archers out in front. The Scots were also in three divisions, commanded by Sir William Douglas, King David and Robert the Steward. Because of the broken nature of the ground and a deep ravine on Douglas' wing they could not face parallel to Neville's army. The initial attack was made by the Scots and when Douglas wheeled to the left to avoid the ravine he mixed with the king's men and the English archers killed many of the Scots by firing into the dense mass of soldiers.

The steward and the rest of the king's forces had some success when they charged, and Neville and Percy were pushed back. The crucial moment had come, and the English horsemen in the rear were ordered forward. The Scots had not expected this charge and reeled back in disorder. Rokeby now fell on Douglas and two Scottish wings were defeated. The king's division was now outnumbered and the arrival of the English reinforcements under Lord Lucy finished the battle. David II was captured

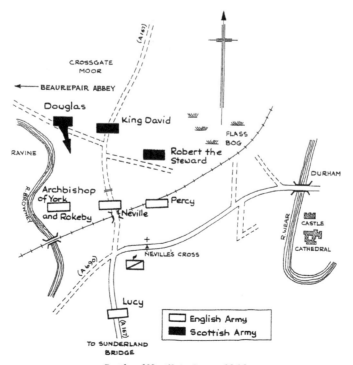

*Battle of Neville's Cross, 1346.*

trying to escape over the Browney Bridge. The following year Percy led a raid into Scotland that met with little resistance.

## Neville's Cross Today

The battle is not named after the English commander but after a more ancient cross, the stump of which is surrounded by iron railings on the right (north) of the A690 (Crook Road) from the centre of Durham, 50 yards (45 metres) before the traffic-light junction with the A167 (the old A1). The ravine and the surrounding country are now significantly built up but the impression of height is apparent from the railway line, which crosses the English position 300 yards (285 metres) north along the A167. A pedestrian footbridge which bestrides the English position has an information panel about the battle. From this one can glimpse Crossgate Moor and the Scottish positions. The ruins of Beaurepair Abbey, where the Scots leaders spent the night before the battle, are worth a visit.

# 40. NEWARK, 21 MARCH 1644

## Nottinghamshire OS Landranger 121 (802 555)

Both sides in the Civil War were anxious for outside help. When Charles negotiated a truce with the Irish to release English forces in Ireland, it was universally

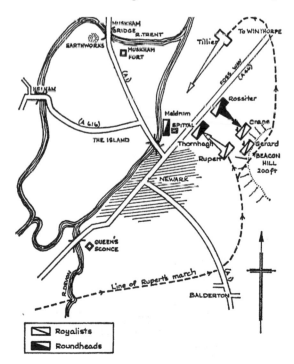

*Battle of Newark, 1644.*

(and inaccurately) believed that Irish Catholic soldiers would also join him. The fear prompted the Solemn League and Covenant of Parliament with the Scots: Scots forces came in exchange for a Presbyterian church in England.

When the Scots invaded early in 1644 the Marquis (formerly Earl) of Newcastle, who had fallen back on York after the defeat at Winceby, found himself besieged by both the Scots and the Roundheads from Hull, and outnumbered.

Charles I soon realised the importance of the town of Newark. It was on the Fosse Way and the governor, Sir Richard Byron, with his garrison in the castle, could protect the York–Oxford road, which was vital to Newcastle's supplies. Early in March 1644 Parliament sent Sir John Meldrum with a force of around 6,500 men to take this vital town.

Prince Rupert, who was training new recruits at Shrewsbury, was ordered by Charles to march to the relief of Newark. Lord (John) Byron came to his aid with the stragglers of the Royalist army that had been defeated by Fairfax at Nantwich. For infantry Rupert had two new regiments released by the truce from Ireland, under Colonel Tillier, an experienced officer. These he ferried down the Severn to Bridgnorth, where he met them with his cavalry and escorted them to Wolverhampton, where 300 troops from Dudley Castle brought the small army up to around 6,000, more than half of which were cavalry.

Approaching Newark from the south-west, Rupert spent the night of 20 March at Bingham on the Nottingham–Grantham road. Newark was well protected by the rivers Trent and Avon and two forts on the Fosse Way, the Spittal and the Queen's Sconce. The Trent to the north-east of the town forms an island. Here Meldrum had his headquarters; his cavalry under Sir Miles Hobart was in the Spittal, which was connected to the island by a bridge of boats. Rupert left Bingham at 2.00 a.m. and, marching through Balderton, occupied Beacon Hill. Meldrum's scouts had seen his approach and the Roundheads were drawn up in two groups with the cavalry in front. Rupert left Charles Gerard's horse as a reserve and sent Tillier to Winthorpe to attack the vital bridge of boats. He gave his right wing to Sir Richard Crane and led his left in

Newark Castle. (Author)

a valiant charge against Thornhagh's horse, who were facing him. On the other flank Colonel Rossiter, who later distinguished himself with Cromwell's horse at Naseby, led a charge up the hill where he routed Gerard's reserve, capturing Gerard himself.

Meldrum now retreated into the island, his guns keeping Tillier's infantry from the bridge. Rupert, whose charge had been successful, heard from a prisoner that Meldrum's supplies were low and decided to starve out his enemy. Sir Richard Byron in Newark led a surprise attack against Muskham fort, which was abandoned, and after his Norfolk regiment had mutinied Meldrum decided to surrender. Over 3,000 muskets and eleven guns were captured and many valuable supplies for the town were obtained. Meldrum's army marched out with their colours and drums but little else. Rupert's victory came at a fortunate time and more than compensated for Royalist defeats at Nantwich and Winceby. His use of river transport for his infantry was novel as well as rewarding, for so often during the Civil War the foot soldiers had to march long distances and were then made to fight on the same day.

Later in the Civil War Newark held out for the king in a long siege, finally capitulating in May 1646.

## Newark Today

Situated on the A1 between Stamford and Doncaster, Newark is more famous for its siege (6 March 1645 to 8 May 1646) than its battle. The actual site of the Spittal is now covered by railway lines, but the Queen's Sconce is well preserved and there are other visible earthworks at Muskham Bridge, Crankley Lane, Crankley Point and Wiverton Hall. A remarkably detailed account of the siege, *Newark on Trent, the Civil War and Siegeworks* (HMSO, 1964) even mentions one John Tredway, who supplied the Royalist garrison with leather and tobacco and in the siege 'was there in person to sell them'.

The National Civil War Centre is open 10.00 a.m. to 5.00 p.m. daily (nationalcivilwarcentre.com) – films, artefacts and modern technology combine for a good day out. There is a bullet-pierced uniform belonging to a Royalist officer on display as well as arms and armour.

# 41. NEWBURN FORD, 28 AUGUST 1640

## Northumberland OS Landranger 88 (165 652)

The reign of Charles I was beset by difficulties from the first, and in Scotland the new prayer book of Archbishop Laud led to the signing of the Covenant and to the first of the Bishops' Wars. Charles seized Scottish ships in English ports and sent Sir Jacob Astley to fortify Newcastle upon Tyne. Berwick-upon-Tweed and Hull were similarly fortified but the loyal Edinburgh Castle was captured by the Scots in March 1639. The Scots had a capable and experienced general, Sir Alexander Leslie, formerly field

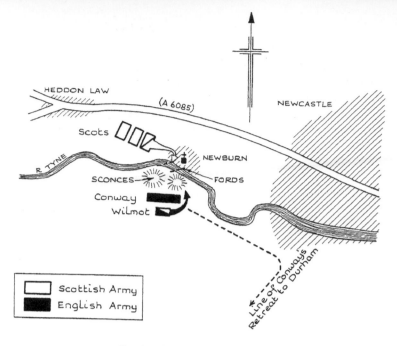

*Battle of Newburn Ford, 1640.*

marshal to King Gustavus Adolphus of Sweden; he trained his men to fight in brigades with musketeers supporting the pikemen. His one weak arm was his cavalry, but his artillery was very effective and, apart from heavy cannon, he developed a German idea of making temporary cannon, two of which could be carried on a single packhorse. The barrels, of small calibre, were made from iron, bound in hide.

The first Bishops' War ended in an uneasy truce at Berwick. The second started when Leslie's regiments crossed the Tweed in August 1640. Lord Conway, who had been attempting to fortify Newcastle, hastily built two sconces at Newburn, a few miles west of the town, where there were two fords accessible only at low tide. There was a small mutiny in the English army when two pence were deducted from the pay of each man for accoutrements. Lord Conway, nevertheless, had 3,000 foot and 1,500 horse to hold up Leslie's Scots until reinforcements could arrive from the king at York.

On the night of 27 August, Leslie was at Heddon Law looking down over Conway's position. The latter had placed his artillery in the two sconces, one of which was commanded by Colonel Lunsford. When a Scots officer appeared the following day to water his horse he was shot down by an English bullet and the battle started. Leslie had placed some of his portable cannon on the tower of Newburn Church. These were skilfully managed and the shot bowled into Lunsford's earthworks, killing many soldiers and causing the rest to flee in disorder.

Lord Hope's son led his volunteers from the Edinburgh law courts across the river, which was just fordable at four o'clock. Then Colonel Blair's musketeers crossed, followed by the Scottish horse. Conway's second sconce was now abandoned and the foot soldiers retired in disorder. The young Henry Wilmot, in command of the English cavalry, then charged the Scottish lifeguards of Sir Thomas Hope's regiment. The Scots yielded and only Blair's flank fire prevented them from being driven back into the river. Lord Wilmot was wounded and captured and Lord Conway's standard-bearer, Charles Porter, was killed and the standard captured. Around fifty were killed on both sides and the fleeing English cavalry trampled down some of their own infantry in a narrow lane. Had someone been able to reorganise them, the Scots might still have been defeated, for only part of General Leslie's army made the crossing, the tide allowing a mere one and a half hours to cross.

Conway fled to Durham and Newcastle was abandoned. 'Never so many ran from so few,' said one writer. The mayor of Newcastle surrendered to a company of Douglas's horsemen on Saturday 30 August, and it was not until August 1641, after being paid £60,000, that Leslie retired to Scotland.

Montrose was present at Newburn Ford and led the vanguard across the ford at Coldstream. He was in charge of the Stirling and Strathearn levies, but the battle was over before they came into action. He fell out with Argyll. He wrote to the king, suggesting he come to Scotland and unfortunately the Covenanters intercepted the letter. He was sent to prison but was released when the king came to Edinburgh, having written no less than three letters to him, but it wasn't until March 1642 that he was released. Leslie, now Earl of Leven, promised the king that he would never again take arms against him.

## Newburn Ford Today

Best approached from the A69 north of the river, Newburn is a suburb of Newcastle where derelict industrial land has been reclaimed as the Tyne Riverside Country Park. The river was altered in the nineteenth century, so nothing remains of the fords, one of which ran diagonally across the river near the present bridge. There is a good view of the river, the bridge and the tower of Newburn Church from the country park. In the Black Gate Museum, Newcastle, there is a cart wheel found at Newburn, no doubt from a cart which did not make the crossing in time.

Below Newburn church is the Boathouse Pub where one can photograph the river. Near here was the ford as the metal bridge was not there of course in 1640. There is a monument inside the Country Park.

# 42. NORTHAMPTON, 10 JULY 1460

## Northamptonshire OS Landranger 152 (759 957)

In October 1459 the Yorkists submitted at Ludford Bridge and a Lancastrian army captured Ludlow Castle. The Earl of Warwick, the Earl of March (later Edward IV) and other Yorkists fled to Calais, thought the Duke of York himself went to Ireland. After raiding Sandwich with a small force strengthened by the addition of soldiers from the Calais garrison. London opened its gates to the Yorkist army, but part of Warwick's force had to be left behind under his father Lord Salisbury to lay siege to the Tower, which was held by the Lancastrians.

Henry VI, Queen Margaret and the Duke of Buckingham were in Coventry collecting an army. From there they moved to Northampton where, just south-east of

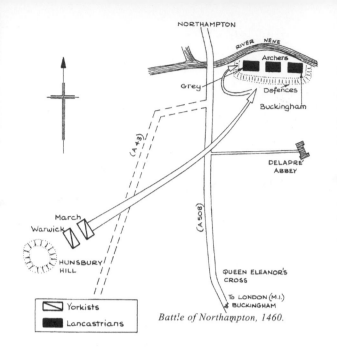

*Battle of Northampton, 1460.*

The Eleanor Cross. (M. Whatton)

the town, they entrenched themselves by a bend of the River Nene facing south away from the river. 'High banks and keep trenches' were thrown up, as Hall's Chronicle relates – the king 'studies nothing but of peace, quiet and solitary life' – so it was left to Margaret and Buckingham to prepare for the battle. Lord Grey of Ruthin, a cousin of the queen, defended the right flank, Buckingham the left, and the archers were in the centre. Edward and Warwick spent the night of 9 July on Hunsbury Hill, where there are still traces of a hillfort. Before it was light they attacked – Edward's men leading – across the Nene marshes to Delapré Abbey. Watching from nearby Queen Eleanor's Cross were the Archbishop of Canterbury and the Papal Legate, who the day before had tried to arbitrate, but without success.

It poured with rain all day and Edward's mounted infantry were stuck in the mud, where they were easy prey for the king's archers. The defending cannon were drenched, but pointed wooden spikes kept the horsemen out. Buckingham had nearly won the day, but suddenly the unexpected happened.

Lord Grey, perhaps influenced by the fact that the Archbishop and the Papal Legate had arrived with Warwick, suddenly ordered his men to lay down their arms. The Yorkists poured over the defences and attacked Buckingham's flank. Behind, the swollen River Nene took its toll on the desperately fleeing royal army. Buckingham, Shrewsbury, Lord Beaumont and Lord Egremont were among the slain. The king was taken to London and lodged at the Bishop's palace, and York came over from Ireland to claim the throne. Queen Margaret and a few Lancastrians escaped to Chester, while in London the council agreed to make York protector and heir apparent during Henry's lifetime.

## Northampton Today

Enter the town by A508 from the M1 junction. On the right before the railway is a large park. At the end of this is Delapré Abbey, now dating mostly from the sixteenth and nineteenth centuries. The Eleanor Cross stands outside the abbey ground on the

Northampton: the River Nene.
(Author)

main road. The actual battle was fought by the river, and the nearest one can get to the site is Nunn Mills Road. The cupola on the stables of Delapré Abbey is just visible from here, but the Archbishop and the Legate must have had very keen eyesight to see the battle from the cross in the middle of a storm. Some of the abbey's rooms are open to the public.

# 43. OTTERBURN, 19 AUGUST 1388

Northumberland OS Landranger 80 (880 940)

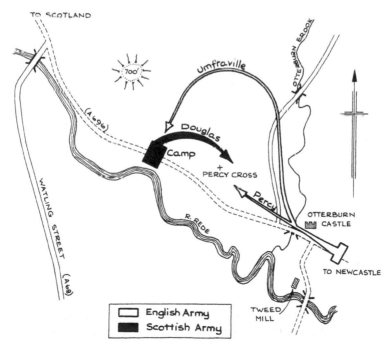

*Battle of Otterburn, 1388.*

During the minority of Richard II the Scots, divided into two armies, crossed the border. The Earl of Douglas, with the smaller army, was beaten off when he had reached Newcastle by Sir Henry Percy, Earl of Northumberland, and his son Henry (Hotspur), who had an army of 7,000 mostly mounted, lightly armed soldiers. Douglas retreated with Percy's lance pennant and young Percy, determined to retrieve it, followed close behind.

Making for the border, the Scots attempted to capture Otterburn Castle in Redesdale. This attempt failed, so they camped in a wood nearby, keeping a sharp lookout for Percy. The latter detected their camp at around midday on 19 August and, dividing his forces in two, decided to attack the Scots while they were resting from their fruitless attacks on the castle. Sending Sir Thomas Umfraville on a wide detour to attack the Scots in the rear, Percy led his main body against their outposts on the slope before the camp. By this time it was dark and Douglas, with his main body, must have passed close to Umfraville without either party seeing the other. Making a flank attack, the Scots fell upon the English and captured the two Percys. In the melee Douglas was killed, but the Scots had other leaders present, notably the Earl of Dunbar, who led his men without his helmet, having had no time to prepare himself because of the surprise of the English attack.

The battle was over by the following morning and Umfraville, who had attacked an empty camp and returned by the way he had come, led the English back to Newcastle, turning to capture several pursuers at one point, while Dunbar led the Scots back to Scotland. The Percys were not prisoners for long and in 1399 they joined Henry Bolingbroke when he landed at Ravenspur to take the throne from the unfortunate Richard II.

Otterburn: the Percy Cross, erected by local landowners in 1777. (ARN Kinross)

## Otterburn Today

The small village of Otterburn is famous for its army camp and its tweed mill. It is 32 miles (51 km) north of Newcastle on the A696 to Scotland. The Percy Cross, which marks the site of the battle, is signposted near the school on the right of the road going towards Scotland. It was erected by the local landowner at the request of the Earl of Northumberland in 1777 and is not a cross but a standing stone on a plinth. There is an interpretation panel by the car park.

# 44. PRESTON, 17–18 AUGUST 1648

## Lancashire OS Landranger 102 (551 321)

After the defeat of Montrose in 1645 the Royalist power in Scotland passed to the Duke of Hamilton, who was a moderate Presbyterian with many friends in England. When the Second Civil War broke out in Wales in May 1648, Oliver Cromwell had immediately set forth for Pembroke, sending General John Lambert to Yorkshire, where Scarborough and Pontefract castles had been seized by Royalists. Charles was a prisoner in the Isle of Wight but he had signed a document known as the Engagement agreeing to a Scottish invasion.

Hamilton, supported by his brother the Earl of Lanark and by the Earl of Callander, raised an army of 10,000 and crossed the border on 8 July intending to make for Wales where, unknown to him, the rebellion had already fizzled out. Cromwell joined Lambert at Knaresborough. They had 'a fine smart army fit for action' of around 8,500. Hamilton had been reinforced by 3,000 men under

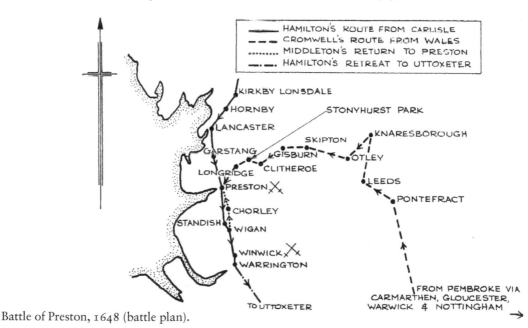

Battle of Preston, 1648 (battle plan).

*The Northern Campaign, 1648.*

Sir Marmaduke Langdale, who was the Royalist leader at Rowton Heath. Another Royalist army from Ulster, small but well-armed, landed in Galloway under Sir George Munro. On 16 August the Parliamentarians camped in Stonyhurst Park, Preston. Langdale, who was leading the vanguard, spotted them and sent to Hamilton for reinforcements, but these never materialised. The Scottish cavalry under General John Middleton was far to the south at Wigan and the infantry were preparing to cross the Ribble when Cromwell attacked. Langdale had placed his troops on a bank overlooking Ribbleton Moor. They checked the oncoming troopers and fought them from hedge to hedge. One detachment of Cromwell's horse reached the bridge before Langdale and only with difficulty did the Cavaliers escape, leaving many dead and several hundred prisoners in the town. Hamilton in person led his own regiment of horse to beat off the Roundheads from the bridge. By crossing at a ford over the Ribble he managed to rejoin the infantry, who had been drawn up on the banks of the Darwen at Walton.

The night was so wet that the Royalist leaders decided to march on to Wigan and join up with Middleton. They marched swiftly, and all the powder wagons were left behind. The orders for them to be blown up were never carried out and Cromwell, who had already captured Hamilton's personal plate, now captured his army's powder. The Royalist cavalry had decided to join up with their foot and the two passed each other at night. Middleton, a former Roundhead, found Cromwell not Hamilton at Walton. The presence of Monro, who was moving slowly south through the Lake District, meant Cromwell had to leave part of his force behind in Preston. Meanwhile Colonel Francis Thornhaugh, pursuing Middleton, was cut off and killed. It was the one Royalist success of the campaign.

On 18 August the Scots, tired, hungry and depressed by the continual retreat, turned at Winwick, where there was a natural defile, and held up Cromwell for three hours. At least 1,000 Scots were killed, and many fled to the church, where they were captured. William Baillie and 2,600 Scottish infantry surrendered in Warrington and only Hamilton and the remaining cavalry carried on south to surrender on 25 August at Uttoxeter. Hamilton was later executed in London. The Earl of Lanark refused to let the English leaders take refuge in Scotland and many were captured. Monro and most of his army returned to Ulster. Colonel James Turner, one of the English Royalists, summed up the defeat: 'The weakness, rawness and undisciplinedness of our troops, our want of artillery and horse … made us prey to Cromwell's army. What was intended for the king's relief and restoration posted him to his grave.'

## Preston Today

The town rises high above the Ribble, and the bridge must have been difficult to capture. There is a dramatic picture of the battle in the Harris Museum in the Market Square. Winwick is just off the M6 (exit 22). The church is fourteenth century, dedicated to St Oswald, but most of the dead were buried at nearby Wargrave, which has a Victorian church. The Walton Bridge of 1900 over the Darwen can be seen today. There is no monument. Another battle took place in Preston in 1715 when Lord Derwentwater's Jacobites barricaded themselves in the centre of the town, where they were soon surrounded by Hanoverian troops.

# 45. ROWTON HEATH, 24 SEPTEMBER 1645

## Cheshire OS Landranger 117 (445 645)

Parliament gained virtual control of the north at Marston Moor, but in September King Charles scored a great victory at Lostwithiel. Returning, he had to face three Parliamentary armies at Reading and, although beaten, managed to escape with most of his army to Oxford. At the beginning of 1645, abortive peace talks were held and Parliament proceeded to organise the New Model Army, which succeeded in preventing Prince Rupert from gathering his forces to invade Lancashire and Yorkshire. In June the great defeat at Naseby in Northamptonshire resulted in the annihilation of the king's army; he was never again able to muster so many. Further Roundhead successes followed fast and the last hopes of Charles were now centred on the Highlanders of James Graham, Marquis of Montrose, but he, having made himself master of Scotland by his victories in 1644 and 1645, was defeated at Philiphaugh on 13 September 1645.

After Naseby, King Charles had only his cavalry in the north to defend him from the New Model Army. Lord Goring was defeated at Langport in Somerset on 10 July and Prince Rupert surrendered Bristol to Sir Thomas Fairfax and was deprived of his commission by the king. The Parliamentary commander in the north was Colonel-General Syndenham Poyntz, a professional soldier recently returned from overseas, whose troop of dragoons numbered 3,000, around the size of the king's remaining cavalry.

Travelling from south Wales via Worcester and Denbigh Castle, Charles arrived in Chester on 23 September, hotly pursued by Poyntz. For the king, Sir Marmaduke

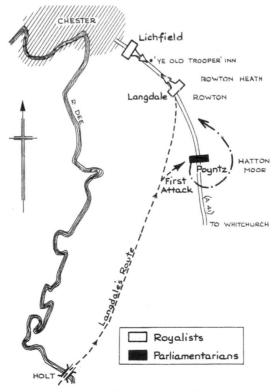

*Battle of Rowton Heath, 1645.*

Rowton Heath: the Old Trooper Inn. (Author)

Rowton Heath: King Charles's Tower on the walls of Chester. (Author)

Langdale was sent over the River Dee at Holt, where the Royalists had constructed a bridge of boats, to attack Poyntz and the army besieging Chester in the rear. At 9 a.m. Langdale, who knew Poyntz's plans from an intercepted letter, charged the Parliamentarians in the flank and drove them off with loss. Poyntz rallied his men and managed to take up a position on Hatton Down near Rowton, where he was in touch with the besiegers, who strengthened his force with 300 foot under the Earl of Lothian and 500 horse under Colonel Jones.

Charles in Chester had sent out a relieving force under Lord Bernard Stuart, Earl of Lichfield, and Lord Gerard. Before they could join with Langdale, Poyntz attacked. His charge drove Langdale back to the walls of Chester, where Gerard and Lichfield stemmed the retreat. 'But the disorder of those horse which first fled,' explains Clarendon, 'had so filled the narrow ways that at last the enemy's musketeers compelled the king's horse to turn and to rout one another and to overbear their own officers who would have restrained them.' The shrewd Poyntz had succeeded in drawing out the cavalry into territory unsuitable for horses for, although Rowton is flat, the narrow lanes nearer to Chester were ideal for musketeers, and the main battle was fought there

Rowton: Horses on the heath. (Author)

rather than at Rowton. Charles, who had seen the battle from the city walls, fell back to Denbigh, leaving behind 800 prisoners and 600 wounded and dead. Among the latter was Charles' cousin, the gallant Earl of Lichfield, who in 1642 had begged permission from Charles to fight with Prince Rupert at the first main battle of the Civil War – Edgehill. His cause lost, Charles finally gave himself up to the Scots in May 1646.

## Rowton Heath Today

Around 3 miles (5 km) south-east of Chester on the A41, Rowton is a suburb of Chester but still retains a few green fields. The modern Old Trooper Inn by the canal bridge is the only thing to remind one of the battle. It seems inconceivable that the king could have seen the action from the city walls. It is more likely that he saw the later rout under the walls, which still stand today. There is no monument.

# 46. SHREWSBURY, 21 JULY 1403

## Shropshire OS Landranger 126 (515 170)

Henry IV (Henry Bolingbroke) seized the throne in 1399, having deposed Richard II with the help of the Percys. The start of his reign was a continuous struggle against rebellions. The Scots were defeated by the Percys at Homildon Hill in 1402 but Owain Glyndwr remained undefeated in Wales, where he was joined by Sir Edmund Mortimer. The elder Sir Henry Percy, Earl of Northumberland, and his son Hotspur demanded that they submit their Scottish prisoner, the Earl of Douglas. But the Percys rebelled, proclaiming that Richard II had been starved to death by Henry and that the Earl of March, Mortimer's nephew, was the rightful heir to the throne. Douglas and Glyndwr planned to join them, and Hotspur moved south from Chester to join up with the Welsh.

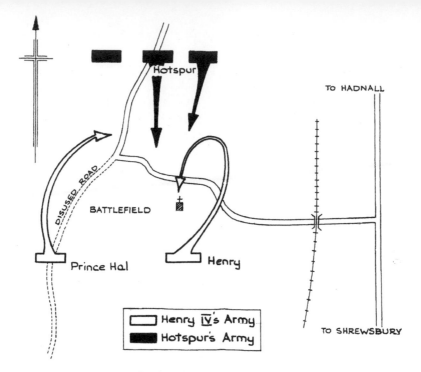

*Battle of Shrewsbury, 1403.*

Shrewsbury: Battlefield church. (M. D. Kinross)

The king's teenage son Henry, Shakespeare's famous Prince Hal, was at Shrewsbury with a small army. The king moved from Lichfield to Stafford and joined his son on 20 July, arriving in time to cut Hotspur off from Glyndwr. Camping for the night at Berwick on the Severn, he discovered that he was in danger of being cut off from Chester by the advancing enemy, so he positioned his army on a slope, now known as Battlefield, some 3 miles (5 km) north of Shrewsbury. Prince Hal's men were on the left and King Henry, with the main force, was on the right. The royal army numbered around 12,000, some 2,000 more than Hotspur's.

Both armies were using the longbow, and the Cheshire bowman soon halted the king's advance. Hotspur attacked on the left wing and centre. Douglas and Hotspur, with a small handful of men, tried to reach out and cut down King Henry, but before they got far, Prince Hal, whose men were getting the better of their opponents, suddenly turned to the right and attacked Hotspur in the rear. Young Hal was wounded but refused to leave the field, and Hotspur was killed by an arrow. The rebels fled, and thus ended 'the worst battle that ever came to England and the unkindest'.

## Shrewsbury Today

Take the A49 out of Shrewsbury towards Whitchurch; after the Market Drayton turning to the right take the first left turn, down a narrow dead-end that goes under the railway. The church is in the middle of the battlefield. The surrounding terrain is mostly flat, but there is a slight ridge at right angles to the railway on the other side of the road to the church – this marks Hotspur's position. The church was founded by Henry IV as a chantry chapel to a nearby college in memory of the fallen. Inside are the crests of the victors. Some of the gargoyles are supposed to represent the rebels.

There is a restaurant (where the church key is kept) an unmanned museum, car park and inside the church some interesting coats of arms of the contestants. Haughmond Abbey ruins are close by and worth a visit. They are opened regularly by English Heritage.

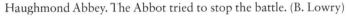

Haughmond Abbey. The Abbot tried to stop the battle. (B. Lowry)

# 47. STAMFORD BRIDGE, 25 SEPTEMBER 1066

East Riding of Yorkshire OS Landranger 105 (720 552)

On the death of Edward the Confessor in January 1066, his successor, Harold, was beset with difficulties. His claim to the throne was challenged by William, Duke of Normandy, who was a cousin of Edward, whereas Harold was only a brother-in-law. In May Harold's rebellious brother Tostig, the exiled Earl of Northumberland, was in arms against him, and in September the king of Norway, Harald Hardrada, suddenly joined forces with Tostig and set sail from his base at Bergen for the Humber estuary.

Harold was watching the south coast with his levies, but early in September he disbanded them and went to London with his house earls. In York Edwin, Earl of Mercia, and his brother Morcar were defeated by Hardrada and his Vikings at Fulford, a few miles south of the city. The invaders had left their ships at Riccall on the Ouse, having sailed up from the Humber. Instead of advancing on defenceless York they returned to their base, perhaps because Hardrada was concerned about his son Olaf, who was in charge of the boats. Harold had set out from London for the north as soon as he had been able to collect an army. Arriving at Tadcaster on 24 September, he entered York the following day. His men were tired, but Harold was strengthened by Edwin and Morcar's remaining troops. The enemy were resting at Stamford on the River Derwent, where arrangements had been made to exchange prisoners. Harold had no intention of resting while his enemy were unprepared for an attack.

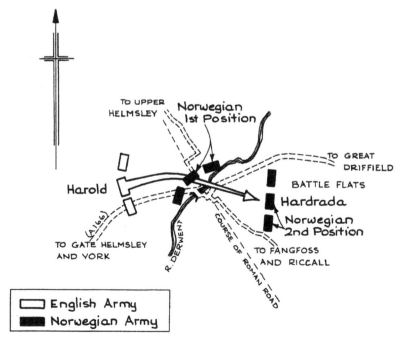

*Battle of Stamford Bridge, 1066.*

The English, numbering around 4,000, attacked the invaders, who were numerically superior, perhaps 5,000, but they had left Olaf with a strong force at Ricall 12 miles (19 km) away.

The Vikings were on both sides of the Derwent, which is around 40 feet (12 metres) wide, and the bridge was several hundred yards upstream from the present bridge. It was built of wooden poles and must have been very narrow. The English charged down to the riverbank, where many of the Norsemen were positioned. The enemy were without their heavy armour, which had been left behind at Riccall, and they reeled back in surprise. Hardrada gave the order to retreat to the Battle Flats, a level piece of ground 50 feet (15 metres) above the river to the east. According to legend, a giant Norseman held the bridge with his axe for at least half an hour while Tostig and Hardrada marshalled their troops and sent a messenger to Olaf for reinforcements. An English soldier found a swill barrel, which he emptied and used as a boat to get under the bridge without being seen. With his long spear he thrust between the poles of the bridge floor at the brave Norseman and wounded him. Harold then led his men over the river and the main battle began.

Deceived by a feigned withdrawal, the Norsemen, who had formed a shield wall, advanced upon the English and a bloody struggle took place. Hardrada was hit in the throat by an arrow and Tostig took over the command. In a brief pause Harold offered his brother his life if he withdrew, but Tostig was playing for time until his reinforcements arrived. The road to Stamford from Riccall is not a comfortable march for heavily armed warriors, and having to fight at once upon arrival was too much for them. The English put them to flight. Only a few escaped to their boats, among them Olaf, who was forced to promise never to attack England again and allowed to sail away with the survivors. Harold had won a famous victory, but at some cost, for his army now had to return to meet a greater foe in the south. On 26 September William landed at Pevensey with a mightier army, determined to capture the English throne.

Stamford Bridge: the battle monument and stone displaying a Norwegian ribbon. (Author)

Stamford Bridge Today

A few miles west of York on the A166 the road climbs to the village of Gate
Helmsley then descends suddenly to the River Derwent and Stamford Bridge. The
old bridge was several hundred yards further upstream, just below the present
weir. Today the river is crowded with caravans on one side and traffic on the other.
A memorial stone pillar to the battle is a bricked seated surround between a car
park and a mill. An inscribed plaque on the wall records the battle. There is only
space for around six cars here.

# 48. STOKE FIELD, NOTTINGHAMSHIRE, 16 JUNE 1487

Nottinghamshire OS Landranger 129 (755 495)

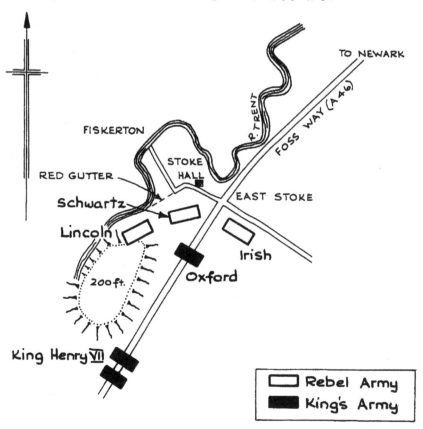

*Battle of Stoke, 1487.*

Just south-west of Newark on the south side of the River Trent is the small village of East Stoke. There is a sudden steep bank to the hill that runs at right angles to the village. It is an ideal defensive position. After Bosworth Henry VII, the final victor for the Lancastrians, was safely on the English throne, but two years later trouble broke out in Ireland. Lambert Simnel, a ten-year-old boy, was proclaimed King Edward VI by the Earl of Lincoln. The earl was a Yorkist by birth and so wealthy that he could hire 2,000 German mercenaries to fight for him. Joined by Lord Lovell, Richard III's former admiral, he landed on the Lancashire coast in June 1487. With Irish reinforcements and discontented northern Englishmen, the total rebel army was around 9,000. Lincoln marched east towards York, which held for the king, then south toward Newark, which was also in royal hands, so he decided to watch both the north and south approaches on the Fosse Way. Henry VII was, by then, closing in on Newark from Nottingham with around 12,000 men.

The Earl of Oxford, a veteran of Barnet and Bosworth, led the royal vanguard, and the rest of the royal army followed in two groups at some distance behind. Lincoln was a shrewd soldier. His line was at an angle to the road so that the opposing army would have to wheel around to get in position. When Henry's army approached in columns, the German troops under Colonel Schwartz, well-armed with crossbows, opened fire. Oxford's men fought hard but made little impression on the rebels until they were reinforced by Henry VII's second and third lines. The 'beggarly, naked and almost unarmed' Irish were the first to break. Many were caught in the narrow Red Gutter, a gully down the steep slope at the west, and others were drowned in the River Trent, 150 yards (135 metres) wide.

The battle lasted for three hours and the German troops fought bravely. Most of the rebel leaders were killed, in spite of Henry VII's order that Lincoln should be spared. However, two of them survived: Lambert Simnel, whom Henry made a kitchen scullion in his palace; and Lord Lovell, who forced his horse into the water at Fiskerton and, so legend says, hid himself in a secret room in his Oxfordshire manor at Minster Lovell. Here a skeleton was found in 1708 when a chimney was repaired. The scene was described by a local historian: 'sitting at a table which was before him, with a book, paper, pen, etc.; in another part of the room lay a cap ... the family and others judged this to be Lord Lovell'.

Henry went to the city of Lincoln to give thanks in the cathedral for his victory. The Yorkist cause was not quite dead. The Earl of Lincoln was one of seven brothers, sons of the late King Richard III's sister, and Henry had married a Yorkist queen, who had other sisters. Stoke Field was the real ending of the Wars of the Roses, and the execution in 1499 of the unfortunate young Earl of Warwick, the last male Yorkist with a direct claim to the throne, closed this chapter of history.

## Stoke Field Today

The village is known as East Stoke, and 3 miles (5 km) south of Newark on A46 the river bends sharply. Stoke Hall stands a quarter of a mile (400 metres) from the bank. The river at Fiskerton does not look fordable, and on the map a ferry – now gone – is marked. When exploring the ground in 1825, the owner of Stoke Hall found skeletons in Red Gutter and near the church. There is a monument against the wall of East Stoke Church, and modern banners hang in the chancel.

Stoke Field: banners
hanging in the chancel
of East Stoke Church.
(R. W. Naesmyth)

# 49. THE STANDARD, NORTHALLERTON, 22 AUGUST 1138

North Yorkshire OS Landranger 99 (362 981)

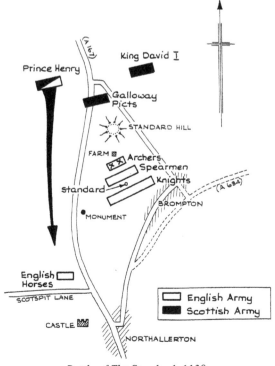

*Battle of The Standard, 1138.*

King Stephen inherited a troubled kingdom in 1135. The Empress Matilda, a grandchild of William I, like Stephen, had an equal claim to the throne, being the daughter of Henry I, and she was supported by King David I of Scotland, who had sworn an oath in 1127 to make her queen of England. He also claimed part of Northumberland as his wife's property and on these two counts led his army of wild Galloway men, pony-mounted cavalry and a few archers to Carlisle, which he soon captured. Moving south-east, he occupied Darlington. King Stephen, meanwhile, was busy in the south, where Robert, Earl of Gloucester, was in revolt at Bristol, and Maminet, Constable of Dover, held Dover for the earl. Beset on all sides, Stephen had but one faithful ally – the Church. His brother was Bishop of Winchester, and the Archbishop of York, Thurstan, was a good friend.

When the invading Scots took the women of Hexham into slavery bound together by ropes, Archbishop Thurstan organised a holy war against the pagan Scots. Men flocked to his enormous standard – a ship's mast topped by a silver pyx containing a consecrated wafer and hung with the banners of St Peter of York, St John of Beverley and St Wilfrid of Ripon. Two of the English army, Robert de Bruce and Bernard de Balliol, who owned land in Scotland, tried to arrange a truce and offered to help the young Prince Henry of Scotland obtain the earldom of Northumberland. It was useless. The two armies, each numbering around 12,000 men, with the Scots possibly the larger force, met on Cowton Moor north of Northallerton (where at that time there stood a Norman castle) at six in the morning. The English fought in three lines, the archers in the front, the spearmen next and the men-at-arms and knights in the third line. In the centre of the middle line the mighty standard stood in an open cart. A mile (1.6 km) or so behind the English line were their horses.

The Scots were in three groups with King David on the left, Prince Henry and his mounted cavalry on the right and in front, at their own request, the wild Picts from Galloway. 'Like a hedgehog with its quills', wrote Ailred of Rievaulx, 'you might see a

Standard Hill Farm. (Author)

Gallwegian bristling with arrows yet still holding his sword'. The Scots' wild charge was checked by the English archers and the well-disciplined foot soldiers, who moved forward to cover the archers as they collected fresh arrows. Prince Henry, seeing the plight of the Galloway men, led a charge round the English left wing and attacked the English horses, the attendant pages and the rearguard. The situation was saved by the English third line, which turned about and encircled the prince. A mighty struggle took place in which the Danes and Normans in the Scottish army fought so fiercely that the retreating king was joined by Prince Henry and escaped to Carlisle without any effective interruption. Old Thurstan and his second-in-command, Walter Espec of Helmsley, were victorious. The bodies of at least 10,000 men were buried in Scotspit Lane. Most of them were Scots. Peace came to Yorkshire, but the battle marked the beginning of King Stephen's civil war, not the end.

## The Standard Today

Leaving Northallerton by the A167, note the monument to the battle by the right-hand side of the road around 3 miles (5 km) to the north. It has an interesting shield depicting the standard mounted on a cart with the banners of the three bishops. There is a Maltese cross at the top representing the archbishop. The Wainwright coast-to-coast walk from St Bees to Robin Hood's Bay crosses the Scots' position. Standard Hill Farm is built close to the centre of the English line.

In Helmsley Church is a stained-glass window depicting the oath sworn on the standard before the battle by Walter Espec and Archbishop Thurstan. Espec's shield shows three spiked chariot wheels.

# 50. TOWTON, 29 MARCH 1461

## North Yorkshire, OS Landranger 105 (479 379)

In 1461 the second battle of St Albans resulted in a Lancastrian victory, and the townspeople of London (Yorkists for the most part) were so alarmed that trade stopped and men buried their valuables. For nine days Queen Margaret did nothing and the young Yorkist leader, Edward, Earl of March, returning from his victory at Mortimer's Cross, arrived in London with the Earl of Warwick and the remnants of the defeated army from St Albans.

The Yorkists were quick to reorganise their army. Lord Fauconberg raised the Kentish Yorkists, the Earl of Warwick brought in supporters from the Midlands and Edward himself made for Pontefract, where the Yorkist army assembled to face the Lancastrians, who were positioned at Towton, 10 miles (16 km) south of York. Edward had declared himself king at Westminster before he left London.

The Lancastrians, numbering (according to Hall's Chronicle) over 30,000, were positioned north of the River Aire, and on 28 March the Earl of Warwick and

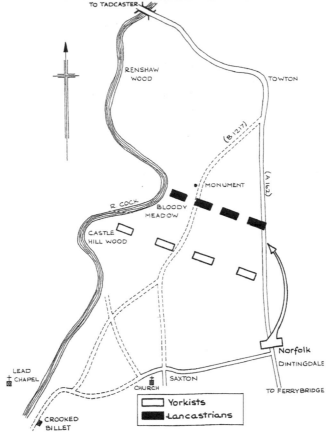

*Battle of Towton, 1461.*

Lord Fitzwalter tried to hold part of the north bank near Ferrybridge against an overwhelming Lancastrian attack led by Lord Clifford. Fitzwalter was killed and Warwick extricated his men with difficulty. Lord Fauconberg with the Yorkist vanguard then crossed the river upstream at Castleford and caught Clifford's retiring force in the flank. Clifford was killed by an arrow and the entire Yorkist army, in numbers slightly less than the Lancastrians, but as yet without the Duke of Norfolk's men, who were on their way from East Anglia, crossed the river and formed a line on a ridge north of Saxton, facing the enemy. Across a slight dip the Lancastrians stood on a similar ridge.

Henry VI did not want to fight on Palm Sunday, but his captains, Northumberland, Somerset and Lord Dacre, took command. The Yorkist Fauconberg, a small, wily experienced soldier, ordered his archers to fire and step back. The strong wind and driving snow were blowing hard at the Lancastrian ranks, so that when their archers returned fire their arrows fell well short.

The Lancastrians now advanced and the Earl of Warwick suddenly found that he was bearing the brunt of the attack. The Yorkists held on grimly. Large numbers of dead and wounded confused and interfered with the battle. On the west flank a group of Lancastrians surprised the Yorkists in Castle Hill Wood and Edward's line began to bend. Two hours after the initial clash of arms Norfolk's men arrived to aid the Yorkists and proceeded to advance on the right wing towards Towton. The Lancastrian left wing was soon outflanked and began to retreat towards the bridge over the River Cock on the Towton–Tadcaster road. The riverbanks are very steep here and it is probable the Cock was in flood. The slaughter at the bridge was very great; also at

Towton: Lord Dacre's cross. (ARN Kinross)

Lead Chapel. (ARN Kinross)

Tadcaster, where there was an attempted stand by a few Lancastrians. At one stage in the battle, Warwick killed his horse as a symbol to his followers that he was staying and they shouldn't abandon the battle. His ruse seemed to have worked, although no doubt the horse wouldn't have agreed.

The casualties in this, the largest battle of the Wars of the Roses, were enormous. King Edward reckoned there were 28,000, but this is no doubt an exaggeration. Certainly the Lancastrians lost the flower of their chivalry. The earls of Devonshire and Wiltshire were beheaded after the battle; Lord Dacre was shot in the head by a bolt from a crossbow while resting with his helmet off during a lull in the battle; Henry VI was ultimately captured and imprisoned in the Tower; the queen and her son fled to France. The battle of Towton ensured the rule of Edward IV but it did not end the Wars of the Roses.

## Towton Today

Take the A64 out of York and turn onto the A162 at Tadcaster. The first hamlet you come to is Towton. Turn right here to Saxton. Lord Dacre's cross is on the hill on the right and dates from the late fifteenth century. In Saxton churchyard is his grave, rather dilapidated but recognisable for its coat of arms showing a quartered chequered shield. In a field opposite the Crooked Billet near the little River Cock is the small Lead Chapel – although it is much older than the fifteenth century, it appears to have no gravestones from the battle. Further up the hill is a farm track, to one side of which are two grave mounds, now barely recognisable as such. The monument has been neatly repaired by an Australian tourist. A 3-km trail has been added recently with interpretation boards and room for four cars at Lord Dacre's cross. We got the last space and saw four of the boards, two across the road marking the position between the two sides. A returning walker, who was covered with mud as if he was a battle survivor, appeared (March, 2016) and saw us safely out of the small car park.

# 51. WAKEFIELD, 31 DECEMBER 1460

West Yorkshire OS Landranger 110 (337 183)

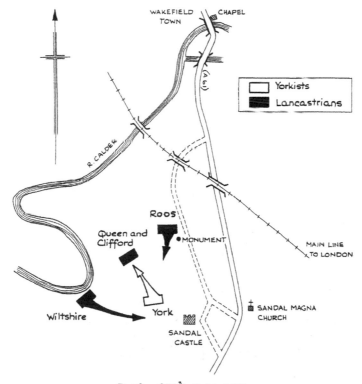

*Battle of Wakefield, 1460.*

The battle of Northampton installed the Duke of York as protector for the third time, but when he claimed the actual throne for himself, many thronged to Queen Margaret's banner in support of Henry VI. The queen's Lancastrian forces concentrated in Yorkshire, so York, advised by Lord Salisbury, set off with an army of 5,000 for the north. Edward, Earl of March, went to the Welsh border to raise reinforcements, and the Earl of Warwick remained in London. It was a fatal decision as the Lancastrians were united at Hull while the Yorkists were divided

After a skirmish at Worksop, York arrived at Sandal Castle outside Wakefield and decided to remain there until his reinforcements arrived. Margaret, with an army of 18,000, approached from York and cunningly posted a detachment of her troops on Sandal Common in full view of the castle. The main body of the Lancastrian army under Lord Clifford was divided into two groups – the foot soldiers under the Earl of Wiltshire and the horse under Lord Roos. Clifford placed them out of sight of the castle.

The ruse worked. York, perhaps faced by the choice of death by starvation or in battle, chose the latter. He may have been taunted by the queen into action but he was naturally impatient and, against the advice of Sir David Hall and old Salisbury, he decided to attack the queen's army. The impact of the Yorkist charge broke the Lancastrian line and a great struggle took place. Clifford did not pause. Sending Roos and Wiltshire into the attack, he caught York 'like unto fish in a net'. Wiltshire captured Sandal Castle, which was undefended, and Clifford caught the unfortunate Earl of Rutland, York's eighteen-year-old son, on Wakefield Bridge, where he killed him outright, having sworn to avenge his father's death at York's hand at St Albans in 1455.

The duke was also killed, along with 2,900 Yorkists. Old Salisbury was taken to Pontefract Castle, where he was imprisoned, only to be dragged out by the Lancastrian mob and murdered. The heads of the Yorkist leaders were stuck on Micklegate Bar in York so that 'York might overlook York'. Lord Clifford had his revenge, but there were two Yorkists left to continue the struggle – Edward, Earl of March, later Edward IV, and his brother Richard, later Richard III.

After the capture of Sandal Castle, only Skipton and Bolton castles remained in Yorkist hands. 'Richard of York Gave Battle In Vain' is the mnemonic used by local children (and some adults) who want to remember the colours of the rainbow.

Wakefield: Sandal Castle. (Author)

## Wakefield Today

The A61 leads out of Wakefield towards Barnsley, and Sandal Magna is the first suburb it reaches. The remains of the castle are at the end of Castle Road. The battle was fought on the field near the entrance. The monument to the Duke of York was knocked down by the Roundheads after Sandal surrendered in 1645, but in 1897 the present memorial was erected in the grounds of Manygates School and has a likeness of the duke based on the statue of him that used to stand on the Welsh Bridge at Shrewsbury. The chapel on Wakefield Bridge, supposed to have been endowed by Edward IV in memory of the Earl of Rutland, was actually built in the fourteenth century.

# 52. WORCESTER, 3 SEPTEMBER 1651

## Worcester OS Landranger 150 (846 525)

In August 1651 young Prince Charles, who had been proclaimed King Charles II at Scone, crossed into England with a Scottish army of nearly 17,000 men under the new

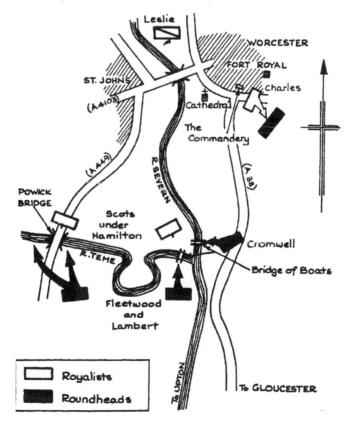

*Battle of Worcester, 1651.*

Duke of Hamilton (brother of the executed duke) and General David Leslie. It was a formidable force, and General John Lambert, hurrying north with his cavalry to Warrington, was quickly sent flying south to Coventry. On 22 August, having advanced via Newport and Wolverhampton, Charles arrived at Worcester.

The Scots had pillaged on their march, and few English joined them. (Ninety-four years later Bonnie Prince Charlie discovered the same thing, and his army was smaller than the Royalists at Worcester.) Oliver Cromwell collected an army of around 28,000 and moved towards Worcester from Nottingham. Lambert seized the Severn Bridge at Upton-upon-Severn and Charles' only remaining escape route was to the north. Charles hastily reorganised the defences of Worcester, relying on the Severn and the Teme, which meet near Powick Bridge, to protect him from Lambert, and Fort Royal with its guns to protect him from Cromwell. Leslie's horse were positioned outside the gates to the north.

Charles Fleetwood's garrison from Banbury had now arrived at Upton, and Cromwell placed him in charge of the western bank of the Severn. Twenty boats were assembled to act as a bridge, which would be floated upstream to form bridges across both Teme and Severn. It was a bold plan, and it succeeded under the noses of the Scottish infantry, who were thrown off balance by a troop of horse that crossed by a ford south of Powick Bridge. Fierce fighting took place here, the spot where Rupert had won his cavalry battle in September 1642. It was also the anniversary of Cromwell's great victory over the Scots at Dunbar, which discouraged Leslie from fighting at all.

Charles, watching from the cathedral tower, possibly saw the bridges quickly assembled and Cromwell crossing with his regiment to consult Lambert and Fleetwood. Noting that the Roundhead right wing was now leaderless and isolated,

The Commandery. (Author)

the young prince gathered all the troops he could find and charged out of the east gate, protected by the guns of Fort Royal. The Roundheads reeled in surprise and a cavalry charge would have routed them, but Leslie still would not move. In spite of all Charles' pleas, the Scottish cavalry fled by the road to the north. Cromwell's reappearance on the right wing in the nick of time had proved his greatness as a general. His regiment forced the Royalists back into the town, where many were killed in the narrow streets. It was 'his crowning mercy' and one of his greatest victories.

One thing marred Cromwell's victory. In the evening light – the battle had lasted five hours and the bridges were not complete until mid-afternoon – Charles escaped with one or two faithful followers to the safety of the Giffords at Whiteladies and Boscobel and ultimately across the Channel.

## Worcester Today

There are very many monuments spread out in the city to see of the battlefield of Worcester because it was not a field battle. Old Powick Bridge still stands, although partially rebuilt in 1837. It is now used mostly by fishermen. One can walk along the banks to the confluence of the Teme and the Severn and see where the bridges of boats were erected. The house where Charles escaped is still standing in New Street. Hamilton's monument is now in the cathedral; he was mortally wounded in the last desperate sally from the narrow Commandery cobbled alley, which remains much as it must have looked in 1651. There is a new monument, unveiled on 2 September 2001 (for the 350th anniversary), by Tam Dayell MP in memory of the Scots who died during the battle – it is at one end of Powick Bridge. Note that the bridge is best approached after coming through the villages of Powick, carrying on towards Worcester, crossing the new bridge then turning left into Old Road. This is if you are coming from Hereford.

Recent additions to the battle monuments in Worcester include a couple of mock artillery pieces on Fort Royal overlooking the cathedral, with two battle posters. More impressive is the metal carving of the last gun, put there by the Royalists but captured and turned on their enemy by Parliamentarians.

*Above*: Powick Bridge, site of the first and last battles of the Civil War. (JSN Kinross)
*Right*: Battle of Worcester: new monument at Fort Royal. (Author)

# SOUTHERN, WESTERN & EASTERN ENGLAND

## 53. BARNET, 14 APRIL 1471

Hertfordshire OS Landranger 166 (248 977)

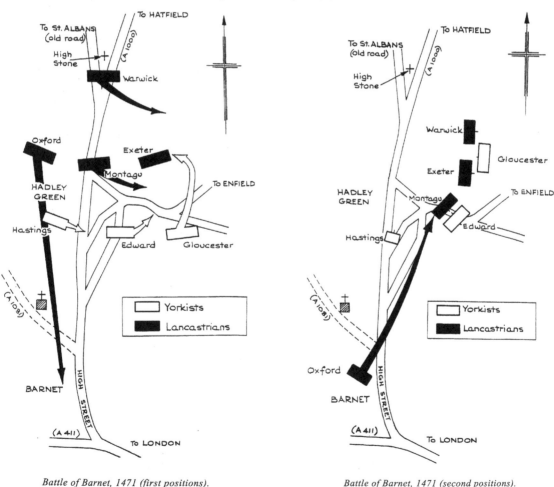

*Battle of Barnet, 1471 (first positions).*          *Battle of Barnet, 1471 (second positions).*

The Yorkists came to power in 1461 after their victory at the battle of Towton. Edward IV, whose father, the Duke of York, had been killed a few months earlier at Wakefield, was crowned at Westminster, but the Lancastrian cause was by no means dead and Edward struggled to keep the country in order. The Earl of Warwick, no friend of the Woodvilles – Edward had married Elizabeth Woodville – plotted with Queen Margaret to put Henry VI back on the throne. He was supported by Clarence, Edward's brother, and the Marquis of Montagu, and Edward found his army outnumbered at Doncaster. On 30 September 1470, accompanied by Richard, his youngest brother, Lord Hastings and Earl Rivers, he escaped to Burgundy from King's Lynn. Henry was king once more and many Yorkists fled for their lives. Edward's brother-in-law Duke Charles of Burgundy lent men and money to Edward to reclaim his crown, and the Yorkist army set sail on 11 March 1471.

On 14 March Edward landed at Ravenspur with a force of French and Flemish troops. Between him and London, where his wife and Yorkist spies were hastily gathering recruits, was the Earl of Warwick, 'the Kingmaker', his former friend, now a bitter enemy. Warwick's army was at Coventry but the earl was anxious to gain reinforcements before he attacked. At the gates of Coventry, Clarence intervened, this time joining his brother with several thousand men and the Yorkists marched south and entered London in triumph. Warwick, the Earl of Exeter and Lord Montagu followed at a distance and set up their positions near Barnet on 13 April, blocking Edward's route to the north.

Time was on Warwick's side, for Queen Margaret was on her way to help him. With Montagu blocking the St Albans road, the Earl of Oxford on the right and the Earl of Exeter on the left, Warwick held a strong position and he placed himself at the rear with the guns and reserve. His army was around 15,000 compared with the Yorkists' 10,000. Edward arrived and positioned his troops at night, so he was not able to see Warwick's position. Richard, Duke of Gloucester, on the right wing thus outflanked Exeter. Oxford outflanked Lord Hastings on Edward's left.

Barnet: the monument and milepost. (Grant)

Easter Day 1471 was very foggy and visibility was down to around 20 yards (18 metres). Both armies advanced, but only Edward and Montagu found each other at first. Neither gave ground, and on the right flank Richard found he had to turn left to find Exeter's flank, where his sudden attack caused both Exeter and Warwick to turn about and face him. Oxford, the most efficient soldier on either side apart from Edward himself, attacked Hastings' flank and pursued some of his men to Barnet and beyond. Meanwhile, Montagu had turned his men to keep in line with Exeter, so that when Oxford rallied his men and returned to the fight, his expected charge on Edward caught the rear of Montagu's troops instead. It was with the cries of 'treason, treason' that Montagu's archers turned and fired at Oxford.

The battle was over. Montagu was killed and his brother Warwick, attempting to walk to his horse in Wrotham Wood, was overtaken by men less heavily armed, knocked down and slaughtered. Oxford escaped north to fight again at another more successful battle – Bosworth Field. Edward was king again, and the unfortunate Henry VI, who was more interested in books than battles, had neither power nor desire to prevent it.

## Barnet Today

Take the A1 out of London and turn right on the A411 to Barnet. In the centre turn left for Monken Hadley and carry on for around a mile (1.6 km) down the High Street to Hadley Green. At a road junction at the far end of the common is a tall monument, the High Stone, erected in 1740, which has been used at one time as a signpost. The simple inscription reads, 'Here was fought the famous battle of Barnet.' To your left, now a golf course, is where the Earl of Oxford attacked; to your right is Hadley Common, where Richard held his ground. In spite of the houses everywhere, there is a remarkable amount of common land here still, and it is not difficult to imagine the Earl of Oxford's troops returning from Barnet to attack by mistake the rear of the Marquis of Montagu's men.

# 54. ASHDOWN, 8 JANUARY AD 871

## Berkshire OS Landranger 174 (535 820)

The importance of the battle of Ashdown, which took place in a year of battles, lies mainly in the fact that it was the only one of six in which the Danes were beaten by the Wessex Anglo-Saxons, and that details of it have come down to us from an account by Bishop Asser of Sherborne, a friend of King Alfred.

King Ethelred of Wessex (not to be confused with 'the Unready', who ruled 100 years later) was surprised in AD 870 by the sudden seizure of Reading by the Danes under their two kings, Bagsac and Halfden. The Danish foraging party was defeated at Englefield, but a direct attack on Reading failed, and Ethelred retreated along the old

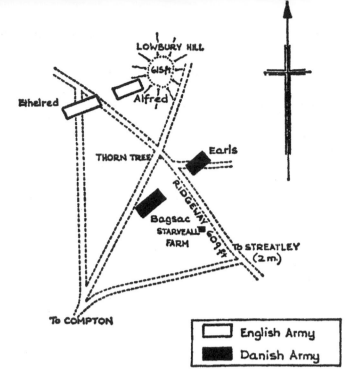

Battle of Ashdown, 871.

*Above*: Statue of King Alfred at Winchester. (ARN Kinross)

*Right*: Ashdown: view of the battlefield. (Author)

Ridgeway, an extension of the Icknield Way running across the top of the Berkshire Downs from Streatley to Marlborough. In the winter of AD 870–71, this track was dry and hard while the valley roads were wet. Thus an army could move quickly only on the high ground. Bagsac soon realised this and advanced on Ethelred, who was awaiting more troops on Lowbury Hill, around 2 miles (3 km) north-east of the present village of Compton and 4 miles (6 km) west of Goring. On the morning of 8 January Ethelred saw the Danish banners advancing towards him, with Bagsac on one side of the Ridgeway and the Danish earls on the other. He divided his army to meet them but did not move. Being a religious man, he chose this moment to order his half of the army down on their knees to pray for a swift victory. Alfred looked on in horror and, according to Bishop Asser, 'he had to choose between withdrawing altogether or beginning the battle without waiting for his brother'. Before losing the advantage of high ground, he charged 'like a wild boar' on the banners of the earls, who retreated to a small hill with a thorn tree, later called Nachedorm ('the naked thorn') in the Domesday Book.

Five of the earls were killed, and the Danes fled back to their camp at Reading. Ethelred's attack later was just as successful and King Bagsac was killed, Halfden escaping with the remainder to Reading. Two weeks later they were in the field again, but the Anglo-Saxons were no longer afraid. They had defeated the invaders for the first time and Alfred obtained a period of peace in Wessex until Ethandun completed his victory seven years later.

## Ashdown Today

Take A329 from Reading to Streatley and turn left on B4009 to Aldworth. Turn right and follow a sign 'To the Down'. The exact position of this battle is not known for certain but the most likely position, after the Saxons had retreated from Reading and assuming they had covered 10 miles (16 km), would be on the old Ridgeway road from Goring towards Wantage, which was one of Alfred's headquarters. Lowbury Hill, which is just on the right of the cross tracks after the farm, is the highest point on Alfred's route, and Starveall Farm, approached by Ambury Road from Aldworth, where the Danes camped before the battle, lies below it, commanding a good view of the Saxon camp. There are thorn bushes around and although the place called Nachedorm is difficult to position, it is most likely to have been in the centre of the battlefield.

# 55. CHALGROVE FIELD, 18 JUNE 1643

Oxfordshire OS Landranger 165 (644 971)

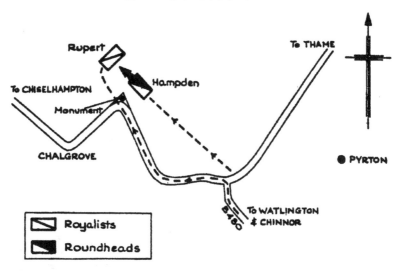

*Battle of Chalgrove Field, 1643.*

Chalgrove today is almost suburban, but behind the new houses Chalgrove Field is still undeveloped and Hampden's monument, erected in the nineteenth century, looks down on the place where he saw his last fight.

On 17 June 1643 Prince Rupert at Oxford received a message from a Roundhead deserter, Colonel Hurry, that a convoy was en route for Thame from London with £21,000 for the payment of Essex's army. Rupert left for High Wycombe via Chiselhampton Bridge with 1,000 cavalry and 500 foot. He arrived too late (the convoy was hidden in a wood), so he turned on Chinnor, set fire to it and captured around 120 Parliamentary recruits.

John Hampden was at Watlington with a small group of horsemen. Realising that Rupert could be cut off, he sent a message to Essex at Thame and with scarcely 200 men he followed Rupert's route towards Chiselhampton Bridge. 'This insolence,' said Rupert, 'is not to be borne,' and, halting his men in a cornfield at Chalgrove, he arranged his cavalry in front with their pistols loaded. Hampden, reinforced by some of Essex's dragoons, led the charge across the corn. The Royalists held their fire until the last moment, when a close barrage from pistols and carbines followed by a charge drove the outnumbered Parliamentarians in all directions. Struck twice in the shoulder, 'with his head hanging down and resting his hands upon the neck of his horse', Hampden rode away towards his wife's home at Pyrton.

It was late and Pyrton was not safe and so, escorted by his lifelong friend Arthur Goodwin, he travelled to Thame, where he was attended by surgeons and a Dr Gyles, sent by the king. Dr Gyles lived at Chinnor parsonage and Hampden had helped design his house before the war. On 24 June Hampden died in a house not far from the grammar school he had attended forty years before. His death was a shattering blow to Parliament. 'I would we could all aly [admit] it to heart,' wrote his friend Goodwin, 'that God takes away the best amongst us.'

Chalgrove Field: Hampden family battle monument. (Author)

## Chalgrove Today

If you ignore the modern houses, this is one of the least changed battlefields of the Civil War. It still has standing corn in June. Taking the A40 from High Wycombe towards Oxford, turn left on the B4009 to Watlington. There turn right onto the B480 to Chalgrove; the Hampden monument is at a road junction. The names of subscribers to the monument are interesting: four of the Fiennes family fought for Parliament, and there are other names well known in 1643. Chalgrove was added to the English Heritage Battlefield Register after its original publication.

Today, Hampden's statue stands in Aylesbury's marketplace, although he probably never stood in such a position with his sword drawn and arm outstretched (at Chalgrove he was mounted with a pistol).

The Victorian monument is close to an aerodrome, but as it is a one-way road and no-through there is safe parking. Chinnor, where Rupert set fire to numerous houses, has a new tea shop inside a bookshop, once a bank with a small car park. This is a pleasantly rural part of Buckinghamshire, a county now under threat of more houses and the High Speed 2 railway to Birmingham.

# 56. CROPREDY BRIDGE, 29 JUNE 1644

Oxfordshire OS Landranger 151 (470 465)

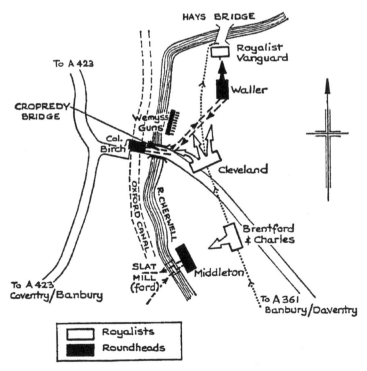

*Battle of Cropredy Bridge, 1644.*

In May 1644 the Royalist garrison at Abingdon was withdrawn to strengthen the king's army, depleted by Hopton's defeat at Cheriton and by Prince Maurice's army besieging Lyme Regis. The Parliamentary commanders were not slow to act. Essex soon captured Abingdon, and Waller guarded the Thames at Newbridge on the road between Witney and Abingdon. Major General Massey moved on Tewkesbury, and to the north there were Roundheads at Eynsham, Woodstock and Bletchington. Oxford was surrounded, and King Charles, advised by the aged Earl of Forth, decided to act. With 5,000 horse and 2,500 infantry, he left Oxford in the evening of 3 June, passing near the Trout Inn at Godstow, crossing the River Evenlode at Church Hanborough and arriving at Bourton-on-the-Water the following day. Essex and Waller followed at a distance until they reached Stow-on-the-Wold, when for some strange reason Essex decided to march to the relief of Lyme, leaving Waller to attack the king.

Charles chose this moment to return to Oxford. At Woodstock he doubled his infantry and collected some guns. To Prince Rupert in Shrewsbury he sent a message to relieve York or, if 'for want of powder' this was impossible, 'to march with your whole strength to Worcester to assist me'. After marching to Buckingham, Charles moved towards Banbury, which was threatened by Waller. On 28 June there was a small skirmish at Crouch Hill near Banbury, which was held by Waller, and the following day Charles marched north towards Daventry, keeping the River Cherwell between himself and Waller.

Thinking that reinforcements were arriving for the Parliamentarians, Forth (lately created Earl of Brentford) sent a small detachment to hold the bridge at Cropredy. Waller was not slow to see the gap in the Royalist forces. He sent his cavalry under Lieutenant General John Middleton across the Cherwell at Slat Mill and attacked the bridge himself with horse, foot and eleven guns. The Royalist van gave way and, reinforced by Lord Bernard Stuart's lifeguards, drew up a barricade further up the river at Hay's Bridge. It was Waller's turn to be caught between two forces. Lord Cleveland's Royalist horse attacked Cropredy Bridge and scattered the defenders, capturing Waller's cannon and their officer in charge, James Wemyss, who had previously been Charles's Master Gunner. With the help of Colonel Birch, who held on to the bridge itself, Waller and his horse escaped, but lost many men and supplies in so doing.

The day was the king's. Waller's army disintegrated, and Oxford was safe once more. Charles wrote to his queen at Exeter to arrange for the christening of his daughter, whom he had not yet seen, but whom he had heard was 'my prettiest daughter'. In July he pursued Essex into the west, leaving Rupert to manage the threat to York. Rupert moved quickly and efficiently towards York and on 1 July he entered the city and the siege was raised. In high spirits, although facing twice his own number of infantry, he forced the battle of Marston Moor.

## Cropredy Bridge Today

Take the A423 from Banbury to Coventry and 3 miles (5 km) north of Banbury turn right to Great Bourton and Cropredy, a small village with a great number of modern houses. The bridge is not the original. There is a small commemorative stone built into the parapet. The fields to the west are much as they must have been in 1644, but the narrowness of the river is surprising – it must have been wider before the Oxford Canal was built.

# 57. CHERITON, 29 MARCH 1644

## Hampshire OS Landranger 185 (597 295)

At the beginning of 1644 the Royalist army under Sir Ralph Hopton, now Baron Hopton of Stratton, had been driven out of Sussex into Hampshire. After a skirmish of Alton in which the Royalists under Colonel Bolle were outnumbered and surrounded in the church, the Parliamentary army of around 8,500 under Sir William Waller attacked the Royalists at Arundel Castle, which was soon surrendered. Many of its defenders subsequently enlisted in Waller's army where the pay was regular and spirits were high.

From Oxford, Charles sent Patrick Ruthven, Earl of Forth, with 2,000 men to Winchester, where he joined the dispirited Hopton. On failing to take Basing House, near Basingstoke, Waller sent his cavalry under Sir William Balfour to Hinton Ampner and followed with his guns and infantry – an army of around 1,000 more than Hopton's force. The Royalist army camped on a horseshoe-shaped ridge between Alresford and Cheriton on 28 March, planning to attack Waller the next day. The guns were placed at the toe of the ridge and a small detachment under Colonel Lisle was on the southern part.

On 29 March Waller attacked through Cheriton Wood, but Hopton's men lined the hedges and fired with such deadly effect that when the Roundheads came through the wood they ran into the Royalist guns which, firing from point-blank range, did a lot of damage. Hopton won the first round, but suddenly a troop of his horse under Colonel Bard charged the horsemen in the field below. They were surrounded by Haselrig's

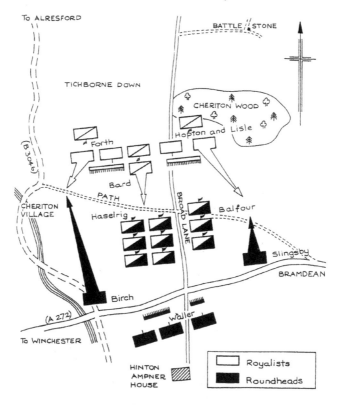

*Battle of Cheriton, 1644.*

Cheriton: the battlefield with Cheriton Wood on the right. (ARN Kinross)

'Lobsters', so called for their armour, and all were killed or captured. The rest of the Royalist cavalry now attacked, one regiment at a time, and met with heavy fire. The king's cousin, Lord John Stewart, was killed, and the popular Sir John Smith was mortally wounded. He was the man who had rescued the colours at Edgehill and his regiment made amends for his death by killing the 'Lobster' who had shot him.

Colonel Birch on Waller's left wing now outflanked the Royalists, who were forced back to Alresford. The town was burnt from one end to the other and in the chaos all the Royalist guns, save two, the baggage and the infantry escaped to Winchester. Hopton and Forth, whose divided leadership had been partly the cause of the defeat, went to Basing House. Waller was suddenly a hero, the London peace party was broken and, in the words of Sir William Balfour, it was 'a great victory over our enemies beyond all expectations'. Royalist hopes of drawing Parliamentary forces south, thus relieving pressure in the north, were gone.

## Cheriton Today

Cheriton is 7 miles (11 km) out of Winchester on the A272. Turn left in the village and, after the River Itchen, take a narrow road to your right. Cross over two farm tracks and, after a left bend, the metalled road forks right. At another junction 1,000 yards (900 metres) further on there is a stone monument on the left-hand side of the road. The track at the foot of the hill by the metal barn leads to Hinton Ampner, where Waller had his headquarters.

# 58. ETHANDUN, AD 878

## Wiltshire OS Landranger 184 (933 523)

In the year AD 871, England seemed a doomed kingdom. Northumbria was occupied by the Norsemen, Mercia was divided between Danes and Anglo-Saxons and only

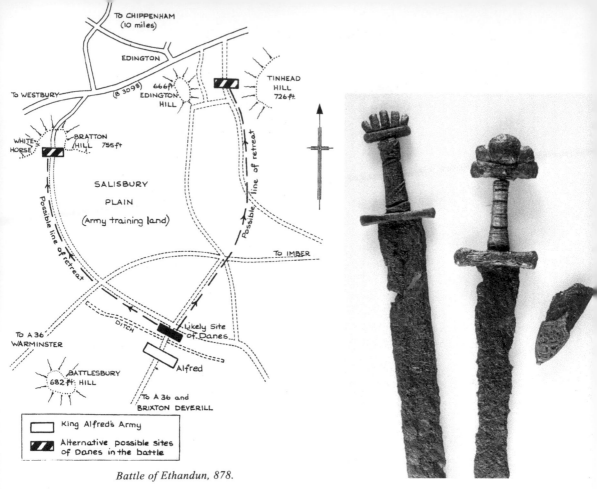

*Battle of Ethandun, 878.*

*Above right*: Viking swords. (National Museum of Iceland)

*Left*: Ethandun: the Westbury White Horse on Bratton Down. (R. W. Naesmyth)

Wessex, or that part of it west of Southampton Water, retained, under King Ethelred, a semblance of order and resistance against the invaders. By the close of the year Ethelred had died and his brother Alfred took over the kingdom. The latter had proved his worth as a soldier at Ashdown and the Danish King Guthrum left him alone for five years until 877, when Exeter was seized by a Danish raiding party from Wareham. Alfred moved to Chippenham, where he held a great feast in celebration of Twelfth Night. Either the sentries relaxed or the storm concealed Guthrum's advancing men, but in the swift battle that followed, Alfred was lucky to escape with a few thegns to Athelney, his hideout on the River Parrett not far from Sedgemoor.

For two months Alfred gathered fresh troops, sending out messengers to Hampshire and Wiltshire for the local fyrds or militias to meet him in May at Brixton Deverill, between Shaftesbury and Warminster. It was a well-known spot because Ecgbryghts-stane, a standing stone near there, was often used as a meeting place. From here Alfred marched to Eastleigh Wood by the River Wylye and, collecting his Hampshire men, he turned north towards Chippenham. The battle of Ethandun or Bratton Down took place on open downland, but Alfred was careful to retain the heights and it was Guthrum's army that had to march out of Chippenham for 10 miles (16 km) and climb up over the down to get Alfred. The Danes had lost their famous raven banner, a silk flag that brought them victory in battle, in an unsuccessful attack a few months earlier against a Saxon strongpoint on Exmoor, and superstition played its part. For hours men fought with sword and axe. According to the *Anglo-Saxon Chronicle*, Alfred 'put them to flight, pursued them as far as their camp and there sat down fourteen days'.

The Peace of Wedmore followed. Guthrum and thirty of his men came to meet Alfred near Athelney, where a great baptismal ceremony was held and the heathens were converted, mercy being shown to the vanquished. According to legend, the Westbury White Horse on Bratton Down was carved by Alfred's soldiers to commemorate the battle. As a result there were fourteen years of peace and England was divided into two zones by a border that roughly followed the present A5. Although there were further battles, the threat to Wessex passed and in the following century the Danes came to England more as settlers than as raiders.

## Ethandun Today

Take the Marlborough–Westbury road (B3098) and the villages of Edington and Bratton are next to each other. Bratton Castle has ditches 15 to 20 feet (4.5 to 6 metres) deep and would be an ideal defensive position. There is a ditch above Warminster that may well be the Danes' first position. Most of Salisbury Plain is Ministry of Defence property, and guns now fire over Alfred's battlefield.

# 59. HASTINGS, 14 OCTOBER 1066

## East Sussex OS Landranger 199 (746 152)

On 25 September 1066 King Harold won the battle of Stamford Bridge, defeating the Viking raiders led by Harald Hardrada, who had landed on a plundering expedition. The very same day William of Normandy set sail from St Valery with 10,000 men and two days later landed at Pevensey. William had met Harold before and had forced him to promise to support William's claim to the throne, which was probably stronger than Harold's because William was a cousin of Edward the Confessor and his great aunt Emma had married Canute. The nearest claimant was Edgar, grandson of Edmund

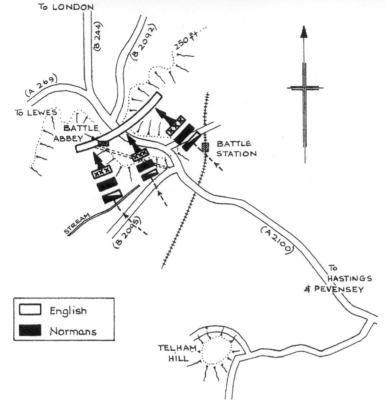

*Battle of Hastings, 1066.*

The site of the battle, looking south from the abbey. (Author)

Ironside and great-grandson of Ethelred the Unready, but as he was a boy the Witan had chosen Harold, Edward's brother-in-law.

The Norman army spent two weeks at Pevensey, which they fortified, not daring to venture far inland before Harold, who had stopped in London to gather fresh troops, appeared on the scene. The English planned a rendezvous in the Weald Forest but many failed to find it, so when their army lined the ridge of Senlac Hill on the London–Hastings road, it was probably fewer in number than the Normans. All through the battle, however, new recruits arrived to take the places of the fallen. The housecarls, Harold's best troops, fought with long-handled axes and spears. Their shields were long and narrow and formed a defensive wall against arrows. The levies fought with any arms they could find – clubs, stones, knives – and some had shields and bows and arrows.

William's knights were dressed in chain mail and rode small horses (see book cover). They were armed with spears and swords and were trained to charge on the flank. When the Norman host approached the long English line split into three groups: the Bretons on the left, William in the centre and the Flemings on the right. The archers, armed with short bows, came on ahead, followed by the infantry and lastly the knights. At first the arrows did no damage and the Bretons' charge was driven back by Harold's right wing. All day the shield wall held and William had to halt to decide on a new plan. His archers had run out of arrows, but messengers had been sent to Pevensey for more. These were fired high and into the back ranks of Harold's army, one of them wounding Harold in the eye. At the same time there was a combined attack from horsemen and foot soldiers. The shield wall broke, the levies fled and Harold was hacked to death. This part of the hill is now marked by the high altar of Battle Abbey.

## Hastings Today

Leave Hastings by the A2100 to Battle, which is 4 miles (6 km) north-west, Battle Abbey, which is open to the public, is on the left and the alter marks the spot where Harold fell. The Normans charged from Telham Hill across the B2095 to the ridge on which the abbey stands. Also on this road is a farm track that follows the original Hasting road northwards and provides a good viewpoint. There are more trees than there were in 1066 and the ground level has risen so much that no relics have been found other than an axe head in Marley Lane. There is an audiovisual display, a battle walk and a car park in Battle Abbey grounds.

English Heritage have moved the memorial stone to Harold by 15 feet, as they now consider the high altar would not have been in the centre of the abbey but on the curved centre of the apse. The public is now able to climb the stairs of the gatehouse to view the battlefield.

There are trains from London to Battle and buses from station. Telephone: 01424 775705. There is a shop and restaurant.

# 60. LANGPORT, 10 JULY 1645

## Somerset OS Landranger 193 (441 271)

The battle of Naseby did not end Royalist hopes, for Lord Goring was in Somerset besieging Taunton with an undefeated army of around 7,000 men. Sir Thomas Fairfax, after capturing Leicester, decided to relieve Taunton, where Colonel Robert Blake was holding out against the Royalists. Marching via Stonehenge and Dorchester, he forced Goring to abandon his positions and form up on the river Yeo near Yeovil, taking care to destroy all the bridges on a 12 mile (19 km) front.

On the night of 7 July the Parliamentary infantry crossed the river at Yeovil and Goring was forced back to Langport. Two days later Goring decided on a rush to divide

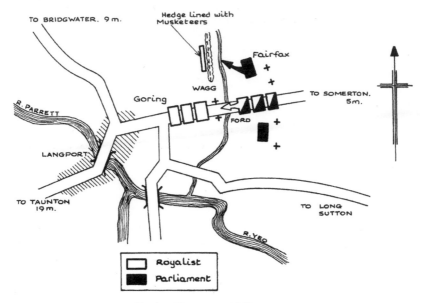

*Battle of Langport, 1645.*

the enemy's strength and he sent his cavalry under George Porter, his brother-in-law, in the direction of Bridgwater and Taunton. Fairfax detached Major General Edward Massey and nearly 4,000 horse in pursuit. There was a skirmish near Ilminster and some of the Cavalier horse were captured. Porter withdrew hastily and Goring had to come out of Langport to beat back the Parliamentary horse.

The Royalists now decided to fall back on Bridgwater, and on 10 July their artillery departed while Goring took up a defensive position at Langport near the hamlet of Wagg. He had returned two guns to guard the road from Fairfax's headquarters at Long Sutton. Musketeers were posted along the hedge and the River Yeo was protected on the right. It was a fairly strong position as the Parliamentary advance would have to march four abreast and cross a ford to get to him.

Fairfax concentrated his artillery on the two guns, which were soon silenced. He then sent his musketeers to attack the Royalist musketeers, and when this succeeded three troops of horse under Major Bethel charged across the ford and into the Royalist horse and infantry, arranged in three lines. Major John Desborough's horse came to the aid of Bethel and on the other flank the cavalry escaped to Bridgwater, which surrendered on 23 July after a struggle. Apart from Prince Rupert at Bristol, western Royalists had virtually ceased to exist and the end was not far away.

## Langport Today

The battlefield is best viewed from the top of Huish Episcopi Church. The Royalists were defending the Wagg Rhyne, and the slope up from the direction of Somerton is the route taken by Bethel. Fairfax's musketeers must have arrived at just the right time to win the day, for Massey's cavalry had rejoined Fairfax after their skirmish at Ilminster. Wagg Bridge, which replaced the form, is a few miles out of Langport on the Somerton Road, B3153.

# 61. LANSDOWN, 5 JULY 1643

Somerset OS Landranger 172 (725 705)

The victory at Stratton ensured the advance of the Cornish Royalists into Devon and Somerset. When their army left Chard on 4 June it consisted of 4,000 foot, 500 horse, 300 dragoons and twenty-one guns. It was commanded by Prince Maurice, Sir Ralph Hopton and the Marquis of Hertford. The headstrong Maurice became involved in a cavalry skirmish at Chewton Mendip, ignoring Hopton's advice to withdraw; he was wounded and captured for a time.

The Parliamentary army had no split command, for Sir William Waller had secured Bath and had been reinforced by Sir Arthur Haselrig's 500 'Lobsters' (musketeers in close-fitting armour). He took up a position on Claverton Down – near the present university – and Hopton sent some of his foot to secure the bridge near Batheaston, but during the night of 3 July Waller crossed the valley in Bath, occupied Lansdown ridge and in the morning opened fire on the Royalist position. Hopton took his army back to Tog Hill via Marshfield. On the afternoon of 5 July Hopton ordered a retreat back to Marshfield; seeing this, Waller sent down Haselrig with 400 horse to attack the Royalist rear. The Cornish foot stood fast and beat them back, and then Sir Bevil Grenville's regiment led the charge up the hill in the face of terrible musket fire. Every piece of cover was used, including a stone wall that gave Grenville's men some much-needed protection. They were supported by Hertford's and the Earl of Carnarvon's horse.

Five Royalist cavalry charges were beaten off, and eventually some of the Royalist guns were dragged up the hill and the Parliamentarians retreated. In the moment of

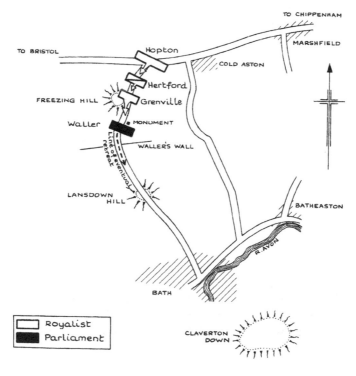

*Battle of Lansdown, 1643.*

victory, Sir Bevil was poleaxed leading a cavalry attack and, according to legend, the giant Payne, his servant, put the thirteen-year-old John Greville on his father's horse and led the final charge on Waller's position. Darkness prevented further fighting. In the morning Hopton discovered that Waller had retreated to Bath and that, at great cost, he had won the day almost entirely because of the bravery of the Cornish foot. Many of his cavalry had fled and, as Slingsby, one of his commanders said, 'Had our horse been as good as the enemy's, the rebels had never gone off the field unharmed.' Lansdown was a temporary victory and it was to be at another action, at Roundway Down, that the Royalist horse were to redeem themselves.

## Lansdown Today

The monument to Sir Bevil Grenville can be found on the left of the road up Lansdown from the A420 Chippenham–Bristol road. It is on the Cotswold Way footpath and is signposted by English Heritage. Further on, where the Ordnance Survey map marks 'earthwork', is a stone wall that may have been the final position of the Parliamentary troops. Waller placed pikes behind this wall and lit torches to deceive Hopton that he was still there before retreating to Bath. From many aspects, the battlefield is not very different from what it must have looked like in 1643.

# 62. LEWES, 14 MAY 1264

## East Sussex OS Landranger 198 (396 112)

When Henry III came to the throne in 1216 at the age of nine he inherited a troubled nation from his father, King John. During the regency the barons regained their power and a new figure emerged. Simon de Montfort, Earl of Leicester, who championed the cause of the new knights and gentry, the poor clergy and the more liberally minded barons against the king. There followed a struggle for the right to control the government of the country, and it was at Lewes that the English Parliament was born.

In 1264, de Montfort gathered a small army of around 4,500 infantry and 500 cavalry and after leaving London made for Lewes, where the king and his son Edward, later King Edward I, 'the Hammer of the Scots', waited with an army twice the size. Between Offham and Lewes, near the present racecourse, Simon placed his army with Henry and Guy, two of his sons, commanding the right, the Earl of Gloucester the centre, the Londoners on the left and his own experienced troops in reserve. On 14 May the king was quartered in St Pancras Priory at Lewes and Edward with the cavalry was in Lewes Castle. Nearly a mile (1.6 km) away, Simon stood ready, anxious to hold the high ground. The royal cavalry charged the left wing and the Londoners fled, taking Prince Edward's force off the field in pursuit for two hours. (There was a similar situation at the battle of Edgehill in 1642). When the king and his brother Richard, Earl of Cornwall, attacked, the forces were more even. 'The king was much beaten

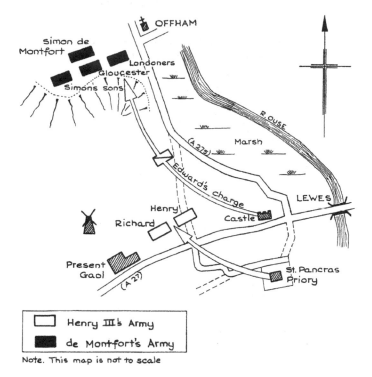

*Above*: Lewes helmet monument. (Author)
*Right*: Lewes Castle: The Gatehouse. (Author)

with swords and maces,' reads a contemporary account; 'two horses were killed under him and he escaped with difficulty.'

Edward returned and captured Simon's abandoned litter or chariot, killing some hostages by mistake and capturing numerous standards. He soon realised that the king had been defeated in his absence, and he retired to confront his father at the priory, losing most of his men on the way. The unfortunate Richard, known as 'the Roman' because he had stood as a candidate in Rome for the imperial throne, was cut off from the king's forces and was captured in a nearby windmill.

Peace was made at the Mise of Lewes, and Henry was kept under guard for fifteen months while Simon set up a parliament consisting of knights from the shires and two representatives from each of the chartered boroughs. Simon had succeeded where the Earl of Essex at Edgehill failed nearly 400 years later. He kept his position and used his forces to defeat his enemy piece by piece with a seasoned reserve as the final shattering blow.

## The Parliament of Knights

King Henry III appealed to his barons in Oxford in 1255 to rescue him from his debts, mostly incurred by foreign wars. Simon de Montfort was the leader of the Council of Fifteen. Leaving their swords at the door, they pledged to 'have the power of advising the King in good faith concerning the government of the kingdom'. It was decided that the king should hold three 'Parliaments' (the word is French in origin) a year – at Michaelmas, Candlemas and in June. Simon took the arrangement as permanent and as he was Earl of Leicester, married to the king's sister, it was not surprising that he became the barons' leader.

## Lewes Today

Take the A27 from Brighton to Lewes and before entering the town turn left on to the A275 to Offham. Walk up the track on the other side of the road from Offham Church to reach Harry's Hill. Simon's position was between some chalk pits on the left and the grandstand of Lewes racecourse on the right. He could see the king's approach from the priory, but Lewes prison blocks the view today. There is little left of the eleventh-century Lewes Castle except the main entrance gateway and keep walls, from one of which one can see the battlefield. A monument in the shape of a knight's helmet stands in the grounds of St Pancras Priory.

# 63. LOSTWITHIEL, 2 SEPTEMBER 1644

## Cornwall OS Landranger 200 (105 597)

After the victory at Cropredy Bridge, King Charles led his army into Devon. The Earl of Essex had relieved Plymouth, which had been besieged by Sir Richard Grenville and his small army of Cornish foot. The two western counties were predominantly Royalist, and Charles' army soon swelled to around 16,000. On 7 August Essex was surrounded at Lostwithiel and Charles summoned him to surrender.

Essex was in a difficult position but he had managed to open his supply line with Plymouth, and the navy was under Parliamentary control. He felt safe enough to refuse the summons, but events rapidly moved against him. On 14 August a force

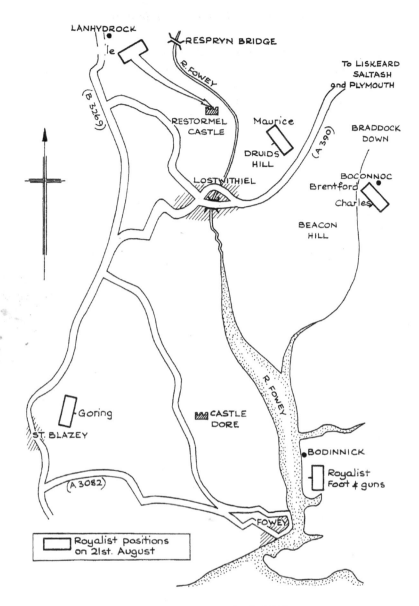

*Battle of Lostwithiel, 1644.*

of 2,000 under Lieutenant General John Middleton, sent by Parliament to relieve him, was defeated near Bridgwater by Sir Francis Doddington.

Charles made his headquarters at Boconnoc, a small village between Liskeard and Lostwithiel, and his army closed in around Essex's 10,000 hungry men. Grenville occupied Bodmin, then stormed Restormel Castle, which the defenders gave up with little resistance. Prince Maurice, who had been besieging Lyme Regis, and the Earl of Brentford (formerly Earl of Forth) occupied Beacon Hill and Druid's Hill on 21 August, while another Royalist troop guarded Respryn Bridge on the Fowey, thus keeping open the communications between Grenville and Charles. On 26 August Lord Goring, who had taken over command of the cavalry from Lord Wilmot, was sent to

St Blazey to prevent Essex moving further into Cornwall. A small group of foot and guns guarded Bodinnick on the Fowey estuary. On 30 August two deserters informed Charles of Essex's plan to embark from Fowey with his infantry and send his cavalry under Sir William Balfour through the Royalist lines.

The main road from Lostwithiel to Liskeard was guarded by a cottage lined with the Earl of Brentford's musketeers. At Saltash on the River Tamar the bridge was broken and Prince Maurice's army was ordered to stand to arms all night. In spite of this, at 3.00 a.m. Balfour's 2,000 horse escaped along the main road, beating off a force on Braddock Down. They crossed the Tamar by boat and, with the loss of around 100 men, reached Plymouth before the Earl of Cleveland and his cavalry could catch them. Undaunted, Charles attacked Lostwithiel. The retreating Roundheads lost two large cannon in the mud, together with other arms and baggage, in the narrow lane to Fowey. Near Castle Dore, Major General Philip Skippon's rearguard made a stand in the evening light. Essex's own brigade recovered some lost ground but the Earl of Northampton's horse drove them back.

Essex now decided to escape. 'I thought it fit to look to myself,' he explained afterwards. He set sail for Plymouth in a fishing boat. After a parley on 1 September, Skippon surrendered the following day. In all, 6,000 men laid down their fight again until they reached Portsmouth, removing their arms and ammunition and capturing forty-two guns. It was his greatest victory of the war, but Charles was too lenient to his enemies and Skippon fought again with his infantry veterans at Naseby.

## Lostwithiel Today

The roads down to Fowey harbour are still narrow and muddy in wet weather. Lostwithiel is a charming old town, fortunately bypassed, and Fowey itself is 'a haunted town made for sailors and pedestrians'. The only remains of Charles' great victory that can be seen today are the earthworks at Castle Dore, near Golant, which date originally from the Iron Age, although they were possibly improved by the Royalists. Restormel Castle is open to visitors.

The block house in Polruan still stands. A cable was run later across the river to a similar blockhouse on the Fowey side but not in the Civil War. Artillery in Polruan would have guarded the entrance to the port.

Fowey Harbour.
The Royalists captured
the blockhouse at Polruan.
(Author)

Lostwithiel Bridge still stands, although the Parliamentarians threatened to blow it up. There is a metal sign near the First and Second World War memorial. The route taken by the Parliamentary cavalry under Balfour that escaped at night through the three Taphouse villages and via Liskeard to Plymouth must have followed the A390. It was a very spread-out battle and the early desertion by Essex did not help morale.

# 64. MALDON, 11 AUGUST AD 991

## Essex OS Landranger 168 (865 055)

For over a hundred years after Alfred, the Danes did not succeed in winning a large battle. Their raiding parties were beaten off or were not of sufficient strength to make any headway. In AD 991, during the reign of Ethelred the Unready, the son of King Edgar, an organised army of Danes and Norwegians descended on Ipswich, which they sacked and, carrying off arms and supplies, the raiders sailed south to the River Blackwater, where they made their headquarters on Northey Island, around a mile (1.6 km) from Maldon.

An epic poem describing the battle has survived. The English leader was Britnoth, a giant of 6 feet 9 inches (2 metres) who was over sixty years old but still a forceful general. He collected an army that was small in number but experienced in battle. Three men guarded the narrow causeway to Northey Island, and until the high tide had ebbed the Danes were powerless to move. Their leader asked for tribute to be paid,

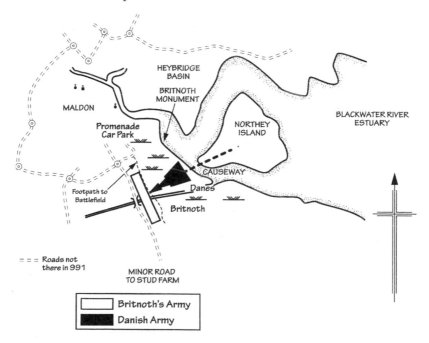

Battle of Maldon, AD 991.

but Britnoth was determined to fight. 'Here stands an earl not mean (small in stature) with this company ... not so lightly shall you come by treasure', he said.

According to tradition, he stepped back and allowed the Danes across the river, but more likely they swarmed over the causeway or crossed in boats and descended on the English. Their archers beat back Britnoth's men and, forming themselves into a wedge formation, they charged. Fighting mostly with spears and swords, the English were overwhelmed, Britnoth was killed and his head cut off by the Danish leader.

Half the English fled, but the three heroes who had held the causeway surrounded Britnoth's body and, joined by a few more, fought on until overwhelmed and killed. The Danes had no more strength left to follow up their victory, but Maldon was the beginning of the Danegeld and Ethelred was forced to pay 10,000 pounds of silver in tribute money. The Danes had come to stay and England was forced to pay for them until 1016, when the Danish king Canute became King of England.

Britnoth was forgotten, but in 1769 a tall skeleton was found in Ely Cathedral. In place of the head was a stump of wax, and from head to foot it was 6 feet 9 inches (2 metres).

## Maldon Today

From Chelmsford take the A414 to Maldon. The battlefield is around half a mile (800 metres) down the B1018 to Latchingdon. A public footpath on the left leads past South House Farm (National Trust). The causeway is marked on Stanford's chart of the Essex rivers as a 'road at low water'. It is about 12 feet (3.6 metres) wide and 170 yards long. The Blackwater river tide approaches it from both sides and if you step off it you sink up to your knees in black slime. No wonder the Danes waited until low water before attacking. It is probable that their ships were too far away as the wharf on Northey Island is further round, facing Heybridge Basin.

There is now a large statue of Britnoth (Byrhtnoth on his statue) at the end of the promenade, where there is a car park. It is by John Doubleday (2006). There is also a mural on the side of the public convenience block and in St Mary the Virgin Church a Battle of Maldon Millennium window by Mark Angus (1991). The causeway can be seen at low tide from the statue and a public footpath lead to the battle site.

Britnoth statue on the promenade. (JSN Kinross)

Newbury I: the Falkland monument.

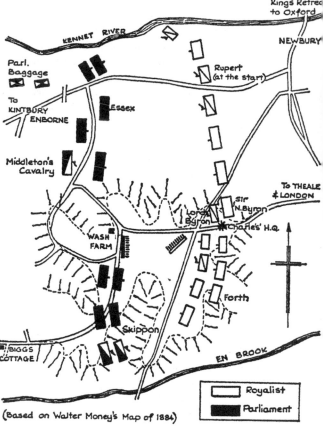

(Based on Walter Money's Map of 1884)

*First battle of Newbury, 1643.*

# 65. NEWBURY I, 20 SEPTEMBER 1643

## Berkshire OS Landranger 174 (455 652)

After the battle of Roundway Down Bristol fell to the Royalists, and in the west only Colonel Massey at Gloucester held out for Parliament. In August Charles laid siege to the city and the Earl of Essex assembled a large army in London to go to Massey's relief. It consisted mostly of the London trained bands, in fact mostly untrained, who were raised to defend London and were paid for by the City. The siege was withdrawn and both sides moved south towards the capital, heading towards Newbury. Charles reached the town first, bivouacked across Essex's path and brought him to battle the following day.

Prince Rupert intercepted Essex's cavalry at Aldbourne Chase and pushed him off the London road, which passed through Newbury. On 19 September the Royalist army occupied the town and Essex camped 2 miles (3 km) to the south at Enborne. The land between the River Kennet and the En brook was more enclosed than it is today.

Commanding the whole position is a 400-foot (120-metre) spur near Wash Farm. The Royalists sent to occupy this were exhausted and spent the night in the farm instead. In the morning Essex's artillery opened up from the hill so that Sir Nicholas Byron's foot below were forced to shelter behind a hedge. His nephew, Sir John Byron, was given the order to clear the hill, which after three charges he succeeded in doing, only to lose most of the ground later in the day. In the first charge young Lucius Cary, Viscount Falkland, Charles' Secretary of State, was killed. His replacement, Lord Digby, was unreliable and had more influence over the king in the fatal years to come.

'The battle,' according to a Cavalier witness, 'was a kind of hedge fight. Neither army was drawn out into the field. If it had it would never have lasted from six in the morning till ten at night.' The Royalist right wing gained some ground, and men on Parliament's right wing gained the highest ground. The young Earl of Carnarvon was killed by a cannon shot and the Earl of Sunderland also met his death. At nightfall the Royalists, perhaps because their twenty guns had used so much ammunition, retired into Newbury and the infantry returned to Oxford, desperately short of powder. Essex was left to continue his march to London, his army badly depleted, for out of about 10,000 on each side at least 6,000 were dead or wounded. 'All were Englishmen,' wrote the Buckinghamshire Roundhead Bulstrode Whitelocke, 'and pity it was that such courage should be spent in blood of each other.'

The following day Prince Rupert could not resist another charge, and the Parliamentary rear were caught unawares near Theale when a squadron of cavalry bore down on them from a narrow lane. In the struggle that followed, Sir Philip Stapleton, finding himself suddenly surrounded, rode up to Rupert and fired his pistol at point-blank range. It failed to go off, and thus ended the most confused and one of the bloodiest battles of the Civil War. As he had failed to destroy the Parliamentary army, Charles could not attempt to take London and contented himself with retaking Reading and Essex withdrew.

Newbury I: Bigg's Cottage, where Essex spent the night before the battle. (Author)

## Newbury Today

Leave the town by the A343 Andover road. Halfway up the hill is the monument to Viscount Falkland, opposite the Gun Inn, which was Charles's headquarters. Turn right, and all the streets have names connected with the battle. The road bends left at Wash Farm. Continue down the hill beyond the bridge, and on the left is the thatched Bigg's Cottage, where Essex spent the night before the battle. There is a stone to the fallen on one of the two tumuli on Wash Common, but the mounds themselves were there before the battle. Fortunately the new bypass does not affect the actual battlefield; the main threat is from new housing.

# 66. NEWBURY II, 28 OCTOBER 1644

Berkshire OS Landranger 174 (464 685)

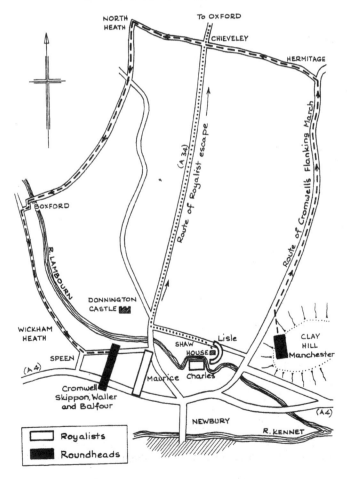

*Second battle of Newbury, 1644.*

The two battles of Newbury were so different that the only connections between them are the antagonists and the town itself. In the autumn of 1644 Charles I returned from his successful Lostwithiel campaign to relieve the sieges of Basing House, Donnington Castle and Banbury. On 19 October three Parliamentary armies united at Basingstoke under the Earl of Essex, Sir William Waller and the Earl of Manchester. Charles' army was outnumbered by nearly two to one but, confident of his communications with Oxford, he relieved Colonel Boys's gallant force in Donnington Castle and sent the Earl of Northampton to relieve Banbury.

On 26 October the Parliamentary army was at Thatcham under the command of a council of war appointed by the London Committee of Both Kingdoms. Essex was ill and Manchester was the senior officer and probably responsible for the dangerously involved plan to send Skippon, Cromwell, Waller and Balfour with almost two-thirds of the army to attack from the west. The route chosen, indicated on the map, involved

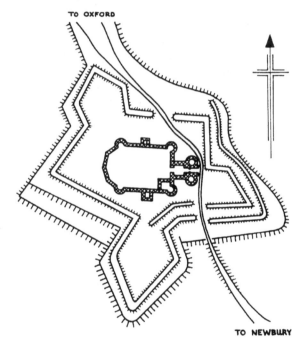

TO OXFORD

TO NEWBURY

Newbury II: ground plan of Donnington Castle at the time of the battle. (R. W. Naesmyth)

Newbury II: Donnington Castle. The earthworks are still visible today.

a night march of 13 miles (22 km) with a bivouac at North Heath. A cannon would announce the attack and Manchester would descend from his position on Clay Hill to attack Colonel George Lisle's men in Shaw House. Charles got wind of the elaborate scheme and sent Prince Maurice – whose brother Rupert was in Bath – to defend the village of Speen with his Roundway Down veterans. He himself remained in the centre with the artillery and reserve horse, his flank protected by the River Lambourn.

The weather was dull and it became dark at 5 o'clock. Skippon's weary men attacked Prince Maurice at 3 o'clock, but Manchester, perhaps confused by Donnington Castle's cannon, did not move. The Earl of Cleveland, who had led the charge that captured the bridge at Cropredy, saved Maurice from being overrun while Boys kept Cromwell, who was strangely subdued, at bay under the guns of Donnington Castle. When Manchester at last attacked the earthworks around Shaw House it was so dark that Colonel Lisle had to remove his coat so his men could see his white shirt. The Roundheads were chased up Clay Hill and in the west Skippon could not get past Speen. During the night Charles withdrew to Bath and his army to Oxford. His men moved so quietly that Charles's enemies were surprised to find next morning that the town was theirs. A week later 1,500 Royalists returned, this time with Rupert, relieved the castle and recovered their artillery, while a small party under Colonel Henry Gage relieved Basing House. There was no third battle at Newbury because Manchester had no stomach for it. 'If we beat the King ninety-nine times he will be King still,' he said, 'but if he beats us but once for the last time, we shall be hanged.'

## Newbury Today

Donnington Castle gatehouse is on the hill at the far end of the village of Donnington. The land around it belongs to English Heritage, which maintains a small car park there. The gatehouse is closed to the public but the ruins are open to all. (The Newbury bypass can just be glimpsed through the trees.) Shaw House, on the east of the A34, is now a school. Above Shaw House is Clay Hill, where Manchester camped. There are no signs of the battle, but it is much easier to visualise than the first battle of Newbury. In Newbury's museum are models of both battles.

# 67. ROUNDWAY DOWN, 13 JULY 1643

## Wiltshire OS Landranger 173 (170 655)

During 1642 fighting went on all over England. The Royalist army in the west was very successful and Sir Ralph Hopton's victory at Lansdown, although a new thing, forced Waller back to Bath. The Royalists moved to Devizes and Prince Maurice, dodging a Roundhead patrol, went to Oxford for reinforcements. Hopton, blinded by an accidental explosion after Lansdown, was so short of ammunition that he had to make some out of resin and bed cord. His men, numbering around 2,500, were weary

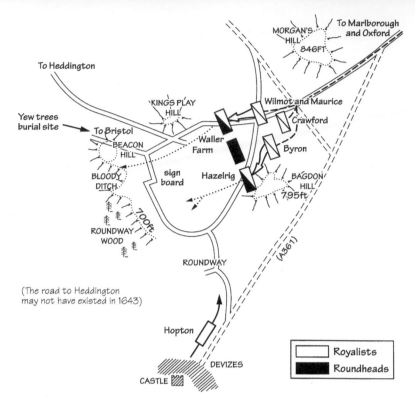

To Marlborough
and Oxford

MORGAN'S
HILL
846FT.

To Heddington

KINGS PLAY
HILL

Wilmot and Maurice

Crawford

Yew trees
burial site

To Bristol

BEACON
HILL

Waller
Farm

Byron

BLOODY
DITCH

sign
board

Hazelrig

BAGDON
HILL
795ft

700ft

ROUNDWAY
WOOD

(A361)

ROUNDWAY

(The road to Heddington
may not have existed in 1643)

Hopton

DEVIZES

CASTLE

Royalists
Roundheads

Battle of Roundway Down, 1643.

and badly armed, but Maurice's relieving cavalry numbered 1,800 and had two small guns. Waller, who had gathered reinforcements in Bath, had around 3,000 foot and 2,000 horse, equally weary but better disciplined. They included Sir Arthur Haselrig's 'Lobsters' and a few cannon.

On 13 July Waller, who had laid siege to Devizes, heard of the approach of Prince Maurice, Sir John (later Lord) Byron and Henry Wilmot. Hopton's men were still in Devizes but Wilmot, who took command as the senior cavalry, officer charged the Roundhead cavalry, which was drawn up on a steep hill near Roundway village. Waller was taken by surprise, for his infantry found no opposing infantry to fight and could not fire at the cavalry for fear of hitting their own men. Haselrig's tin men had time for one stand before they were driven down the steep hill. Waller's cavalry tried to escape through a gap by Beacon Hill, only to find a 300-foot (90-metre) precipice, down which most of them fell.

Roundway Down: the scarp above
Bloody Ditch. (R. W. Naesmyth)

Meanwhile Hopton's Cornish infantry, warned in advance of Wilmot's approach by a prearranged gun signal, climbed out of Devizes and fell on the leaderless Roundhead infantry. Over 600 were killed and about twice that number were wounded and captured, together with all Waller's guns, ammunition and baggage. It was an amazing victory and even a Parliamentary officer remarked: 'We must needs look upon this as the hand of our God mightily against us, for it was He only that made us fly.'

The Royalist tide now reached its peak. On 26 July Rupert captured Bristol, and the western garrisons all fell to the Cavaliers apart from Lyme Regis and Poole. In Kent, where there was very little action in the Civil War, a Royalist rising threatened London, where the hand of John Pym was losing control. But Royalists in the north, east and west were reluctant to converge on London while Hull, Plymouth and Gloucester were in Roundhead hands, so Charles tried to encourage them and open the road to South Wales by laying siege to Gloucester. Realising the psychological importance of this city's resistance, the Earl of Essex and the London militia set out to relieve it. 'Runaway Down' had been a significant victory but the forces taking part were too small for it to have any lasting effect on the war.

## Roundway Down Today

Take the A361 from Swindon to Devizes and Roundway is the village up the hill to the right just before Devizes. The land is now cultivated except for Morgan's Hill and its adjacent golf course. The best view of the site is from King's Play Hill, which is reached from Heddington village near Calne. Beacon Hill's slopes are still as steep as in 1643. Bagdon Hill (now called Roundway Hill) and Morgan's Hill flank the position of Waller's army. The roads are mere tracks, but there is a picnic site overlooking Bloody ditch, where Waller's cavalry came to grief.

The battle plan shown on the site shows Wilmot's left wing going down the hill and back up it again in pursuit of Haselrig's cavalry (the Lobsters). I disagree with this as Maurice and Wilmot fought together with Byron and Crawford on the other wing.

Haselrig survived to become one of the leaders of the Rump parliament. Lord Wilmot played a leading role in getting Prince Charles to the continent after the Battle of Worcester.

# 68. ST ALBANS, 22 MAY 1455

## Hertfordshire OS Landranger 166 (149 072)

The Wars of the Roses, which started with the battle of St Albans in 1455, were a series of disjointed conflicts between the rival families: the reigning Lancastrians and the Yorkists under Richard, Duke of York. The Hundred Years' War in Europe had come to an end and England was full of ex-soldiers who were kept in the pay of the large landowners. While the archers, pikemen and knights never put down their arms, the Wars of the Roses

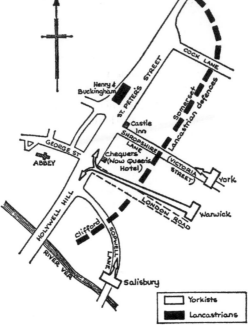

*Battle of St Albans, 1455.*

were a private quarrel, and the ordinary country folk went about their work on the whole undisturbed by national events. The Lancastrian King Henry VI, deeply religious, was not powerful enough to keep order, but in 1455 he shook off a fit of insanity and reinstated Edmund Beaufort, Duke of Somerset, as his chief counsellor, sending his disgruntled cousin, Richard, Duke of Somerset, to Yorkshire. Many considered that York's right to the throne was as good as Henry's and, aided by the powerful Earl of Warwick, Richard marched his army of 3,000 veterans of the French wars south towards St Albans.

Somerset and Henry collected a force of around 2,000 and moved out of London to Watford and St Albans, which they reached just before Richard. Barricades were thrown up in Sopwell Lane and Victoria Street, the royal standard being set up in St Peter's Street. The first Yorkist attack was held up at these barricades by Lord Clifford and the Duke of Somerset. Warwick led his troops between the two streets along the line of the present London road and, finding no resistance, turned left and right to attack the rear of the barricades. Somerset was killed outside the Castle Inn and Clifford died bravely at the barricade; Stafford, son of the Duke of Buckingham, who had tried to make peace before the battle, and the Earl of Northumberland were also killed.

The Yorkist victory was complete, but the captured Henry was still treated as king, and the victorious Yorkists went down on bended knee to kiss his hand. The governing council was reorganised, and there was peace for around four years, but Henry's French queen, Margaret, who had taken sanctuary with her son in St Albans Abbey, was determined to raise the Lancastrian standard once more. Before war broke out again there was an attack from an unexpected quarter. The French raided Sandwich in Kent, and Warwick was despatched to sea to defend the realm. There was a brief reconciliation and the sons of the defeated Lancastrians walked hand in hand in a procession with the Yorkists to St Paul's Cathedral, led by York and the queen. It was only a token gesture, but for a moment the queen's French blood was forgotten and her party grew in strength.

In 1461 another battle was fought at St Albans in which Queen Margaret got her revenge. It was a larger and very different affair and Warwick, who had been the victor of the first battle, was lucky to escape with his life.

## St Albans Today

St Albans is one of the oldest towns in England, and the shape and direction of its main streets have not changed since 1455, with the exception of the London road, which is new and follows the line of Warwick's advance. A plaque on the building at the corner of St Peter's Street and Victoria Street records the death of Somerset.

# 69. SEDGEMOOR, 6 JULY 1685

## Somerset OS Landranger 182 (355 361)

In June 1685, the Duke of Monmouth, illegitimate son of Charles II, landed at Lyme Regis with a handful of supporters, declaring his uncle James II, who had been king for only four months, to be a usurper, and claiming the throne for himself. The West

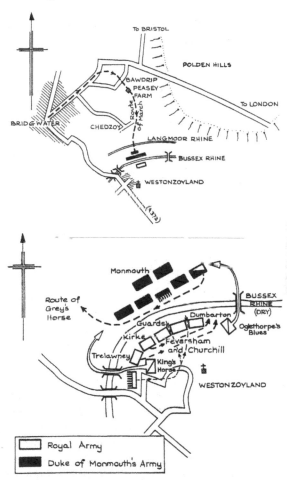

*Above*: Edgar Bundy's 'The Morning of Sedgemoor', 1905. ( © Tate, London 2015)
*Right*: Battle of Sedgemoor, 1685: (above) Monmouth's route from Bridgwater and (below) the plan of the battle.

Country puritans, who had cheered the duke on his tour several years before, responded to his call, and an army of around 4,000 men was assembled that included 800 horse under Lord Grey of Warke and four cannon under Dutch gunners. The King's army was commanded by a Frenchman, the Earl of Feversham, but its second-in-command was John Churchill, future Duke of Marlborough, and two of its regiments were the redoubtable Kirke's Lambs, newly returned from Tangier.

After failing to capture Bristol but defeating a royal force at Norton St Philip, Monmouth camped in Bridgwater on 3 July. Feversham followed at a distance, slowed down by his seventeen cannon, and reached Westonzoyland on 5 July. An outpost of royal cavalry under Sir Francis Compton occupied the village of Chedzoy and another under General Theophilus Oglethorpe occupied Bawdrip. The cannon covered the Bridgwater road, so Monmouth had either to attack or retreat.

He decided on a night attack and the weather helped him for it was foggy as well as very dark. A local guide, Godfrey, led his army in a long, narrow column out of Bridgwater on the Bristol road until they turned right to Peasey Farm, where the ammunition carts were left. Both of Feversham's outposts were avoided, by luck rather than judgement, and the Langmoor Rhyne, a ditch of some 17 feet (5 metres) in width, was being crossed when a shot rang out. The rebels were discovered, and Grey's horse promptly attacked the front. It was a bold move but Bussex Rhine, another deep ditch a mile (1.6 km) away, prevented it. James's army lined one side and the rebels the other. A firing battle went on all night, the rebel artillery taking toll of Dumbarton's Regiment of the Guards, until it ran out of ammunition. Meanwhile, Grey's inexperienced horse had galloped across the enemy front and disappeared until the end of the battle, which came with the daylight. The Bishop of Winchester, a former soldier who was an interested spectator, lent his horses to the frustrated royal gunners and six guns bore down on the unfortunate rebels, deciding the day.

Monmouth, Grey and a few others escaped to the Polden Hills and the infantry, mostly armed with scythes and billhooks, were rounded up or killed on the moor by Kirke's Lambs. Monmouth was later captured and executed, but Grey was pardoned, despite Judge Jeffrey's Bloody Assizes.

## Sedgemoor Today

Take the A372 south-east from Bridgwater and turn left at Westonzoyland. Follow the signs to the battlefield. It is confusing because the Bussex Rhine no longer exists and the ditch you see is modern. There is an interpretation board by Bussex Farm and there are reminders of the battle in Westonzoyland Church. An excellent model of the battle is in the Admiral Blake Museum, Bridgwater.

### The Amazing Escape of Dr Henry Pitman

Henry Pitman and his younger brother, William, were Quakers from Sandford Orcas on the Dorset/Somerset border. Henry had trained as a doctor in Italy and had a deputy job in Yeovil. When they heard of the Monmouth rising the two brothers went to Bridgwater and Monmouth appointed Henry as his surgeon. He treated the wounded from both sides, but after Sedgemoor was captured and his horse stolen. He and his brother were imprisoned in Ilchester Jail (now no longer, but once the principle county jail) and tried at Dorchester. They were transported on the *Betty* from Weymouth to Barbados, then sold as slaves to Robert Bishop.

Badly treated, Henry decided to escape. His brother died, but with five other rebels he joined two debtors and made for the island of Tortuga off the coast of Venezuela in an open boat. They had an early escape when the boat was nearly discovered before they left, but they hid it under water so that they had to bail it out continuously when they were under way. At Tortuga, they had to live off fish and turtle eggs as there was no other food. They managed to survive and eventually an English privateer landed at the island and took off Pitman; the others did not want to leave so were left food and clothing. The ship took Henry to New York, which had recently been taken over from the Dutch, and then he took another ship back to Southampton. When he arrived he discovered that both he and his brother had been pardoned on 31st May 1687.

Henry settled in London, where he wrote and published his account *A Relation of the Great Sufferings of Henry Pitman*. Strangely the good doctor's adventures were not yet finished as he went back to Barbados as a free man and died there two years later in 1693. What became of the rebels left on Tortuga is unknown, but very few transportees returned and Pitman was one of the only men to write an account of their adventures. It must have been read by Daniel Defoe, who was also involved in the Monmouth Rising, but managed to avoid capture. Defoe used it, along with the account of William Dampier's rescue of Alexander Selkirk from Joan Fernandez island, as a source for *Robinson Crusoe*.

# 70. STRATTON, 16 MAY 1643

Cornwall OS Landranger 190 (072 229)

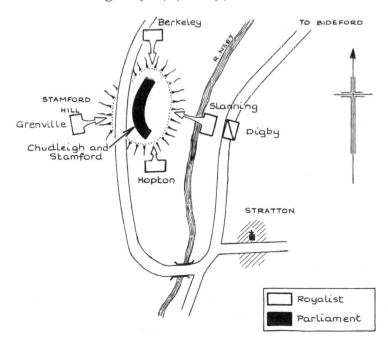

*Battle of Stratton, 1643.*

Stratton: the monument on the battle hill. (D. Sargeant)

The battle of Braddock Down in January 1643 established the Royalists in Cornwall. Sir Ralph Hopton defeated Colonel Ruthin largely because of a gallant charge by Sir Bevil Grenville's Cornish foot. However, Plymouth was strongly held by Parliament and the Royalist Cornish-trained bands decided not to cross the border into Devon. So, with Plymouth supplied by sea, it looked like stalemate.

On 22 April, after a temporary period of truce, James Chudleigh, the twenty-five-year-old son of Sir George Chudleigh, took command of the Parliamentary forces from the Earl of Stamford, who was sick with gout. He had over 2,000 men and decided to attack Launceston, where Hopton was drawn up with around 1,200. Throughout the day the Parliamentarians tried to attack the bridge, but Hopton was reinforced and eventually turned the tide, pursuing Chudleigh to Okehampton. At night the Royalist advance was ambushed at Sourton Down and 1,000 muskets were captured, together with Hopton's correspondence. The latter then withdrew to Launceston and on 15 May Stamford, now recovered, crossed the Cornish border at Stratton, sending Sir George Chudleigh and the Parliamentary horse to Bodmin to interrupt a muster of Royalist-trained banks. Camped on a hill near Stratton, now known as Stamford Hill, the earl imagined himself in an impregnable position, but events were to prove otherwise.

Hopton, whose army was reduced to around 3,000, decided to get between Chudleigh and the earl. He camped outside Stratton and early on 16 May advanced on the hill, which was fortified with cannon and an earthwork. He divided his army into four groups under Grenville on the south-west, Slanning on the east, himself on the south, and Digby with the cavalry on the east, also charged with protecting the road from which the Parliamentary horse was expected. The Royalists could make no impression on the earl's position and by three in the afternoon they were left with scarcely four barrels of powder.

Concealing his shortage of powder from his men, Hopton gave the order for a general charge with pike and sword alone on four sides. The few remaining Parliamentary horse under Stamford escaped, and James Chudleigh rallied his foot to push Grenville and Sir John Berkeley back down the hill, but he pressed on too far and was captured. In forty-five minutes the four parties had met on the hill and the remaining Parliamentarians were put to flight by their own cannon. A total of 1,700 were captured with all the baggage, including £5000 and seventy barrels of powder.

Stratton was one of the most remarkable victories of the Civil War for either side. The Cornish infantry and their commanders proved invincible. Such was their effect on young Chudleigh that he changed sides, and a few weeks later his father resigned his Parliamentary commission. Hopton joined forces with Prince Maurice, Prince Rupert's younger brother, in June at Chard. Sir John Berkeley, who later escaped to the continent and became head of the Duke of York's household, was raised to the peerage as Baron Berkeley of Stratton. His companion, Sir Bevil Grenville, fought on to July 1643, when he met a legendary soldier's death at Lansdown (see page 129).

## Stratton Today

The village of Stratton lies a few miles inland from Bude on the north coast of Cornwall. There are earthworks still visible on the hill and a monument to the battle on the side of a bridge. There is also a plaque on the Tree Inn in the village.

The battle was fought at Poughill off the A39. Pass the hotel and there is a seat by the road – opposite is Bevill House. You are now at the top of the hill and a gate in the bank to the left of the house leads to an arch and a monument.

The old monument is down by the church on the side of the Tree Inn and reads, 'In this place the army of rebels under the command of the Earl of Stamford received a signal overthrow by the valour of Sir Bevil Grenville and the Cornish army on May 16th, 1643.' The pub sign shows the giant Antony Payne who fought for Grenville here and at Lansdown. Opposite the inn is a free car park.

# 71. TEWKESBURY, 4 MAY 1471

## Gloucestershire OS Landranger 150 (890 318)

On the same day as the battle of Barnet, Henry's queen, Margaret, and her son had landed at Weymouth with a small but desperate band of Lancastrians. Edward IV heard the news two days later and promptly organised his army at Windsor. Although short of arms and equipment, Margaret found both at Bristol, where she was warmly welcomed, but few men joined her ranks. North of Bristol, Margaret realised that Edward would prevent her reaching her supporters in Wales. She sent her vanguard to Sodbury Hill, where they created enough disturbance to convince Edward that he should spend the night there and prepare for battle in the morning. The following morning a scout gave Edward the news. It was now a race for the river, and Edward's scouts won. The gates of Gloucester were closed and Margaret's tired soldiers struggled on to arrive at Tewkesbury on 3 May.

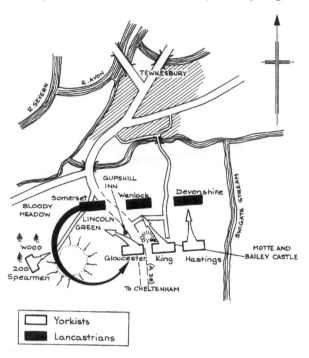

*Above left*: Battle of Tewkesbury, 1471.

*Above right*: Tewkesbury Abbey. (Author)

Jasper Tudor, Earl of Pembroke, was hastily gathering a Lancastrian force in Wales but before it could appear the battle of Tewkesbury was fought. Near Gupshill Manor, Margaret placed her centre under Lord Wenlock, a soldier who had fought for the Yorkists at Towton and was unreliable. The right wing was commanded by the Duke of Somerset and the left by Devonshire. Her force was slightly larger than Edward's army, which was arranged in three groups commanded by Richard, Duke of Gloucester, Edward himself and Lord Hastings.

On 4 May the two armies were about 400 yards (365 metres) apart, but between them on the ground was a mass of 'evil and deep dykes'. Horsemen would be in trouble. Somerset, who had reconnoitred the ground, worked out a bold plan. He led his troops, concealed behind a small hillock, and descended on Richard of Gloucester's rear. It was a brilliant move, but Edward had positioned 200 spearmen in the woods by the hillock and as soon as Somerset passed they attacked his rear, causing so much confusion that Somerset's men were surrounded and defeated.

In the centre Lord Wenlock, accompanied by Margaret's son Prince Edward, was keeping his ground when he suddenly found an angry Somerset beside him accusing him of cowardice and treachery for failing to support the right wing. Before Wenlock could reply, Somerset struck him dead with his mace. The centre now collapsed and the Lancastrians fled for the river and the sanctuary of Tewkesbury Abbey. Young Prince Edward was overtaken by Clarence, Edward IV's brother, and was killed before he could reach the abbey. Somerset was executed the following day with all the Lancastrian leaders, and in London King Henry IV, 'the melancholy spectator' who had survived for so long, was murdered in the Tower.

## Tewkesbury Today

Take the turning to the right after the abbey marked Lincoln Green Road and Bloody Meadow is on your right. The Battle Trail can be reached from here. Much new building has taken place since the original edition of this book was first written. The hillock where Edward's spearmen hid must be in the golf course.

There is a plan at Bloody Meadow, one in the bar of Gupshill Manor Inn and a model with flags and coats of arms in Tewkesbury Museum. Gupshill Manor is on the A38 to Gloucester. It is difficult to accept that this building dates from over forty years before the battle. On the other side of the A38 are Queen Margaret's camp and the earthworks of a motte-and-bailey castle. In Tewkesbury Abbey there is an inscription to the young Prince Edward in the centre of the nave.

The museum is open Tuesdays – Fridays 1.00 p.m. to 4.00 p.m. and Saturdays 11.00 p.m. to 4.00 p.m., from March until August. Telephone 01684 29290; www.tewkesburymuseum.org. It has a diorama of the battle. The town was decorated with banners of the nobles who took part when we called in June (see 'The Street Banners of Tewkesbury').

Tewkesbury battle banners.
(Author)

# BIBLIOGRAPHY

Ackroyd, P., *Civil War: The History of England Vol III* (MacMillan, 2014)

Adair, J., *Cheriton 1644 –The Campaign and Battle* (Kineton: Roundwood Press, 1973)

Anon. *Scottish Battles* (Newtongrange: Langsyne Publishers, 1985)

Barrett, C. R. B., *Battles and Battlefields in England* (Innes, 1896)

Blaauw, W. H., *The Barons' War* (Lewes: Bell & Daldy, second edition, 1871)

Buchan, J., *Oliver Cromwell* (Hodder & Stoughton, 1934)

Buchan, J., *Montrose* (Edinburgh: Nelson, 1928)

Burne, Colonel A. H., *Battlefields of England* (Methuen, 1951)

Burne, Colonel A. H., *More Battlefields of England* (Methuen, 1952)

Carter, A. and J. Stevenson, *The Oxfordshire Area in the Civil War* (BBC Oxford, 1972)

Coate, M., *Cornwall in the Great Civil War* (Truro: Bradford Barton, 1963)

Chandler, D., *A Guide to the Battlefields of Europe* (Wellingborough: Patrick Stephens, 1989)

Chandler, D., *Sedgemoor, 1685* (Anthony Mott, 1985)

Dunning, R., *The Monmouth Rebellion* (Wimborne: Dovecot Press, 1984)

Fuller, J. FC, *Decisive Battles of the Western World* (Paladin, 1970) (Hastings)

Gardiner, S. R., *History of the Great Civil War (4 volumes)* (Longman, 1901)

Gaunt, P., *The Cromwellian Gazeteer* (Stroud, 1987)

George, H. B., *The Battles of English History,* (Flodden, Dunbar: London, 1895)

Guest, K. and D., *British Battles.* (Mayer/Collins, with English Heritage, 1996)

Hallam-Baker, C., *The Battle of Flodden, Why & How* (Remembering Flodden Project, 2012)

Kinross, J. S., *Walking and Exploring the Battlefields of Britain,* (Newton Abbot, David & Charles, reprinted 1993)

Laffin, J., *Brassey's Battles* (Oxford: Pergamon Press, 1896)

Lange, A., *A History of Scotland* (four volumes) (Edinburgh: Blackwood, 1900)

Parry, T., *A Church for Bosworth Field* (Privately published, 1998)

Prebble, J., *Culloden* (Sidgwick & Jackson, 1961)

Robson, J., *Border Battles & Battlefields* (Rutherford: Kelso, 1897)

Royal Commission for Historical Monuments, *Newark-on-Trent – The Civil War Siegeworks,* HMSO, 1964.

Ross, C., *The Wars of the Roses* (Thames & Hudson, 1976)

Rowse, A. L., *Bosworth Field* (Macmillan, 1967)

Seymour, W., *Battles in Britain* (two volumes) (Sidgwick & Jackson, 1975)

Skidmore, C., *Bosworth, the Birth of the Tudors* (London, 2013)

Smurthwaite, D., *Battlefields of Britain* (Webb & Bower, 1984)

Tewkesbury Battlefield Society, *The Street Banners of Tewkesbury* (2013)

Tomasson, K. and F. Buist, *Battles of the '45* (Batsford, 1962)

Warner, P., *British Battlefields* (four volumes: 1.South; 2 North; 3 Midland; 4 Scotland) (Reading: Osprey, 1972–75)

Woolrych, A., *Battles of the English Civil War* (Pimlico, 1991)

Young, Brigadier, P. and J. Adair, *Hastings to Culloden,* (Bell, 1964)

Young, Brigadier, P., *Marston Moor, 1644* (Kineton: Roundwood Press, 1970) (Reissued by Windrush Press, Moreton-in-Marsh in their *Great Battle* series.)

Young, Brigadier, P., *Edgehill, 1642* (Kineton: Roundwood Press, 1967)

Young, Brigadier, P., *Naseby, 1645* (Century, 1985)

Various battlefield guides, especially *The Bosworth Experience* (2012)

## Useful Addresses

Requests for information should always be accompanied by a large stamped, addressed envelope.

*Battlefield Register:* c/o English Heritage, the Engine House, Five Fly Avenue, Swindon SN2 2EH. www.englishheritage.co.uk

*Battlefield Trust:* 16 Friary Meadow, Bury St Edmunds, IP37 6EJ

*Company of Ordinance Artillery 1350-1750:* Colin Armstrong, 20 Deerhurst Way, Swindon, SN5 8AF. www.company-of-ordinance.org.uk

*English Civil War Society:* www.ecws.org.uk

*National Association of Re-enactment Societies:* www.nares.org.uk

*National Civil War Centre:* Newark, Nottinghamshire, NG24 1JY, (01636 655777,) www.nationalcivilwarcentre.com

*The National Trust,* Heelis, Swindon, Wilts, SN2 2NA (01793 817400)

*The National Trust for Scotland,* 5 Cultins Road, Edinburgh EH11 4DF (0844 493 2108) www.nts.org.uk

*Sealed Knot Society:* The Sealed Knot, Burlington House, Botleigh Grange Business Park, Southampton, Hampshire, SO30 2DF www.sealedknot.org

For information on annual re-enactments, contact English Heritage, Engine House, Fire Fly Avenue, Swindon, Wiltshire SN2 2EH. Telephone for special events: 01793 414600

# INDEX